Chris Paul: The Inspiring Story of One of Basketball's Greatest Point Guards

An Unauthorized Biography

By: Clayton Geoffreys

Table of Contents

Foreword

Since his selection as the fourth overall pick of the 2005 NBA Draft, Chris Paul has emerged and solidified himself as an elite NBA point guard. Armed with an incredible basketball IQ and a variety of skill sets as a reliable point guard, Chris Paul has an effect on players around him similar to that of Steve Nash, whenever people play with Chris Paul, they can expect inflated statistics as Chris makes them even better players. Chris Paul is a widely respected point guard throughout the NBA due to his ability to pass the ball from anywhere on the court; beyond this, CP3 also has the ability to score at will and to take over a game when he needs to do so. Now a member of the Los Angeles Clippers after spending his first six years with the New Orleans Hornets, Paul has emerged as the team leader of "Lob City" and has been the large reason why the Los Angeles Clippers are no longer an irrelevant NBA team but instead a legitimate title contender. Thank you for downloading *Chris Paul: The Inspiring Story of One of Basketball's Greatest Point Guards*. In this unauthorized biography, we will learn Chris' incredible life story and impact on the game of basketball. Hope you enjoy and if you do, please do not forget to leave a review!

Also, check out my website at claytongeoffreys.com to join my exclusive list where I let you know about my latest books and give you goodies!

Cheers,

Clayton Geoffreys

Visit me at www.claytongeoffreys.com

Introduction

What if Chris Paul is the greatest point guard in NBA history? Such an assertion seems completely and utterly absurd because Lakers legend Earvin "Magic" Johnson won a total of 5 NBA championships and 3 MVP awards. Johnson revitalized the NBA with the high-octane, flashy offense of the Showtime Lakers, and had one of the greatest sports rivalries with Larry Bird. Even ignoring Magic, Oscar Robertson averaged a triple-double in a single season, and John Stockton leads all NBA players in assists by a ludicrous margin. Gary Payton came as close as any individual player had to stopping Michael Jordan in the 1996 NBA Finals, and even Steve Nash has led some of the greatest offenses in NBA history. So how could anyone assert that Chris Paul, a point guard who has never been past the second round of the NBA playoffs and has never won an MVP, is the greatest point guard in NBA history?

However, among basketball analysts who are fans of newer forms of statistical analysis beyond the traditional box score, there are those who believe such a bold statement. Tom Haberstroh, an ESPN insider who handles those newer "advanced" statistics such as Player Efficiency Rating (PER) and Win Shares, has observed that Paul's numbers are overall higher than Magic's. For example, Paul's career average PER, 25.59, is the 6th highest in NBA history and surpasses Magic's average of 24.11. He has accumulated 115 Win Shares over his first nine seasons while Magic had only 104 over his first nine.

Haberstroh argues that these numbers show that Paul is, in fact, a better point guard than Magic. While Magic does have more rings and MVP trophies, Haberstroh argues that this is because Magic got to play with Hall of Fame players such as James Worthy and Kareem Abdul-Jabbar, unlike Paul, whose team used to be the NBA's doormat and has emerged only in the last three seasons. It is possible that Haberstroh is just a journalist seeking attention with a controversial headline. However, Houston Rockets general manager Daryl Morey, one of the leaders in the NBA's advanced statistical revolution, has also stated that he believes Chris Paul is indeed greater than Magic Johnson.

Could Haberstroh and Morey be right? Most people think otherwise; however, the fact that such an assertion could be made of Chris Paul shows just how good he is. He has sat atop the point guard throne for the past several years, ever since his breakout third season as a pro, and he has become the yardstick for the league's finest court generals. His 2008 campaign was an incredible performance of basketball skill and winning that would have garnered him an MVP award in other basketball years had it not been for the equally amazing year Kobe Bryant had. In his career, CP3 has averaged about 19 points and ten assists per game. He was the 2006 Rookie of the Year, an 8-time All-Star, an All-Star MVP, an All-NBA Team member seven times (four selections with the First Team), and an All-Defense selection seven times. His personal achievements as well as his consistent appearance atop the assists and steals column have all contributed to his campaign as one of the top point guards in NBA history.

Since CP3's breakout year in 2008, younger and more athletic points guards have been asserted one after another to be the one who will finally dethrone Paul, from Deron Williams to Derrick Rose, Russell Westbrook, Damian Lillard, and now to the current MVP, Stephen Curry. Year after year, Chris Paul remains standing atop the list of point guards. His ridiculous court intelligence and handles give him an advantage that no athleticism can beat. On top of that, Paul has the competitive edge and the drive as a leader that point guards younger and bigger than him could not contend with. As Chris Paul continues to lead his team in the upcoming season, the biggest question to ask is: Will his incredible advanced statistics finally lead the Los Angeles Clippers to the NBA's Land of Promise?

Can he help the Clippers, traditionally the most hapless team in the NBA, if not all of sports, win their first-ever championship ring? It is impossible to know the future, but if any point guard in NBA history could lead the Clippers as their undisputed franchise player, it would be Chris Paul.

Chapter 1: Childhood and Early Life

Many NBA athletes have had the misfortune of growing up in broken families and rough neighborhoods, forced to turn to basketball as a way to leave the ghetto and move up in the world. Chris Emmanuel Paul had none of those problems. He was born to Charles Paul and Robin Jones on May 6, 1985, in Winston-Salem, North Carolina. Charles and Robin had known each other since they were children, and the middle-class family supported and loved Chris as well as his older brother, CJ. Robin's father, Nathaniel Jones, bound the family together. Nathaniel opened a Chevron station during the Civil Rights Movement in 1964. It was the first service station run by a black man in North Carolina, and it was in operation throughout Paul's childhood. Affectionately known as "Papa Chilly" throughout the community, Nathaniel was a generous and exceptional man. He was always willing to lower prices or even give away his merchandise to those in need.

Chris's father, an avid fan of the Dallas Cowboys, played football when he was in high school, and both parents did their part in ensuring that their sons led an active, athletic lifestyle. But CP3 did not inherit his father's love for football, though he did play the sport at one point in his life. He got his athletic genes from his mother's side, as Papa Chilly was a good basketball player in his youth.

When Chris was as young as three years old, Charles set up a Fisher-Price plastic hoop for him to play with, and he also coached Chris's youth basketball and football teams. Two years later at the age of 5, Chris would receive his very first basketball. It was a symbolic moment in his life. That basketball gave him the confidence to go out there and play to his heart's content without having to share the ball with anyone else if did not want to.[i]

Far too often, some parents end up playing too active of a role in their child's activities and thus end up spoiling any desire to play sports. Charles and Robin did no such thing and helped their sons keep perspective whenever they lost. At home, Paul's parents were tough, but fair. They made sure their children had good grades, did not use foul language, and went to church. In hindsight, Chris observed that his parents truly supported him as a child with love and kindness. And when things got a little rough between parent and child like in any other family, Grandpa Nathaniel was there to hold the Paul family together.

Chris and CJ loved their "Papa Chilly." The brothers routinely worked at their grandfather's Chevron station, changing oil filters and filling up customers' tanks. Chris and CJ raced each other to incoming cars, competing to be the first to fill the vehicle and get tip money. In the meantime, Chris talked with his grandfather about anything and everything. He considered Papa Chilly to be his best friend and observed that it was his grandfather who taught him the value of hard work.

Papa Chilly was not the only basketball idol that Chris Paul looked up to as a kid. Like most young boys that have had a chance to see and play basketball during the 90's, CP3 was a huge fan of Michael Jordan.[i] He loved how Jordan changed the game of basketball and how he carried himself both on and off the court. Best of all, Paul was a fan of Mike's legendary competitive spirit, which the former would later inherit.

Chris was also very close with CJ—so much so that it sometimes turned into a one-sided tightness of brothers. Though CJ loved his younger brother, he was a little irritated with Chris at times because the younger Paul followed his older brother wherever and whenever he could. As such, CJ's friends never liked the child CP3 very much because they found him annoying. Nevertheless, the Paul brothers maintained a close relationship.

The brothers played youth sports, but Chris was then better known for his football rather than his basketball prowess. He was small as a child, which limited what he wanted to do on the court. As most people know, height is always an important factor in playing basketball, and Paul's size hindered him from playing basketball at a high level early in his life.

To this day, it seems that Chris Paul still has that "little man" complex and always tries to prove himself on the court despite his size. Being short at such a young age helped Chris because it was how he was able to develop the same competitive edge he has always had in his career. Because of this, Chris turned to football. On the football field, Paul's smarts, speed, and leadership more than made up for his size. Chris was widely known for his refusal to back down and his competitiveness, but C.J. was viewed as the superior sports talent and was the better Paul concerning basketball.

However, Chris Paul would still often look at basketball as his sanctuary and domain while growing up. His height was always the biggest obstacle he had to overcome when he was growing up, but it never fazed him from loving the game more. CP3 lived and breathed basketball even at his young age that it never mattered to him how short he was.[i]

Chapter 2: High School Years

When Chris Paul entered West Forsythe High School, he stood at just about 5'1". If that was not problematic enough, C.J. was the starting point guard on the varsity team and the star of West Forsythe. All of Paul's intelligence and will could not compensate for the fact that he was too small to guard anyone. Confident that he could develop, the future elite NBA point guard spent his first two years in high school playing for the junior varsity team. Moreover, Paul never even thought he could make it onto West Forsythe's basketball team because he was then a better football player and at his height, he just could not compete with the bigger teenage guards. Despite playing for the junior varsity team, Paul was a prized player because he was so quick, smart, and competitive that every fiber of his game made up for every inch that he lacked on the basketball court.

In Chris Paul's junior year, things began to turn around. Paul had grown about ten inches over his years on the junior varsity team, giving him the needed height at nearly 6 feet tall. C.J. had graduated from high school and was on his way to Hampton University and then to USC on a basketball scholarship. The door was wide open for Chris to become the new star of West Forsythe, and he delivered. He averaged 25 points, five assists, and 4 steals a game in his junior year and led West Forsythe to the semifinals of North Carolina's 4-A championship. Even though his team lost, Paul still earned the Central Piedmont Player of the Year award. Just like that, Paul went from being just another high school point guard to being one of the biggest high school prospects in the country. With his leadership, ball-handling skills, and passing ability, few doubted that he would be a star in college basketball someday.

Universities from across the Atlantic Coast Conference (ACC) flocked towards Paul in the hope of signing him, but he was quickly attracted to Wake Forest. He had grown up in the university's shadow and was a huge fan of the team. He made an oral commitment to Wake Forest in his junior year, and routinely showed up there to work out and practice. On November 14, 2002, Chris Paul signed his letter of intent for Wake Forest. Paul's entire family, teachers, and friends were there to see him sign and congratulated him, but no word of appreciation meant more to Paul than Papa Chilly's. Paul's grandfather frequently closed his Chevron station to watch Chris play in high school. When Paul signed his acceptance letter to Wake Forest, Papa Chilly took off a Wake Forest hat that he owned and gave it to his grandson. It was one of the happiest days of Paul's life.

It was the last time that Chris would ever see his grandfather. The very next day while Chris was at a football game, Papa Chilly was murdered by a gang of teenagers who sought nothing more than the "thrill" of robbing a helpless old man. Looking for a way to honor his grandfather's memory, Paul devised a plan. He decided that in his next game, he would score 61 points, one point across his name on the scoreboard for each year that Papa Chilly had lived. Even Paul could not help but admit that the plan was slightly ludicrous since his career high with West Forsythe was just 39 points. But he went out and did it. In the second quarter alone, Paul had 24 points, and West Forsythe had the game all but wrapped up by the end of the third. Paul stayed in, and with less than two minutes to go, he had 59 points. He drove to the hoop, scored, and was fouled. North Carolina's high school record for points in a game was 66, and Paul could have gone for that in the last few minutes. Instead, he intentionally missed the free throw to stay at 61, and then left the game because the number was more symbolic than even a hundred more points. He collapsed into his father's arms and sobbed. It was a heartfelt performance for a young star trying to commemorate his close relationship with his grandfather. Paul's accomplishment, tribute, and the love had for his deceased grandfather[ii] made national headlines.

Throughout his senior year, Paul showed himself to be one of the best high school basketball players not just in North Carolina, but the entire country. He averaged an incredible 31 points, eight assists, six steals, and 5 rebounds a game. While he failed to lead West Forsythe to a title again, he was nominated to the McDonald's All-American Team and was voted as the North Carolina High School Player of the Year in 2003. In many other years, Paul would have been the best high school player in the country, but a big teenager by the name of LeBron James was making national headlines with his high school play. Had Chris received the same hype and attention that LeBron had, he would have been an NBA draftee fresh out of high school.

Off the basketball court, Paul was a well-liked and charismatic individual in his high school and served as the class president his entire time in high school. Being a high school class president proved to be a good experience for Chris Paul because it helped him develop into a team leader whose charisma and ability to lead by example cannot be overstated. Even today, Paul returns to West Forsythe to chat with the students there about the value of hard work and proper leadership in achieving success.

Outside of West Forsythe, Paul also showcased his basketball skills in Amateur Athletic Union (AAU) basketball. In his junior year as the star of the Winston-Salem Kappa Magic, Paul won the 2002 National U-17 AAU championship, taking home the MVP award. Between his high school graduation and his arrival at Wake Forest, Paul also played in the McDonald's All-American game alongside LeBron James on the Boys East team. The two future stars put on a show of passing excellence with lob after lob to each other as well as to future NBA players Charlie Villanueva and Jackie Butler. The East pummeled the West behind the two stars. Paul had ten assists and received the sportsmanship award right before taking the drive to Wake Forest.

Chapter 3: College Years at Wake Forest

Freshman Year

Wake Forest is a university with a long history of basketball excellence, but the school had struggled for a few years after the departure of Tim Duncan in 1997. They had been led by future NBA All-Star Josh Howard for the past few years and had reached the second round of the NCAA tournament the previous year. But Howard graduated and moved on to the NBA in 2003, which meant that as the 2003-04 college basketball season began, the Wake Forest Demon Deacons were looking for a new star to lead them. Coach Skip Prosser was confident that the newly arrived Chris Paul would fit the bill as an immediate impact player. He had observed that as a high school player, Paul "was as pure a point guard that you could find" and noted Paul's unselfishness and leadership. That meant that Paul was a once-in-a-lifetime kind of a point guard who knows how to play the position at the highest level possible. But would Paul be able to fulfill the lofty expectations placed upon him?

Paul's levelheaded demeanor ensured his success. In his debut college game against Memphis, he scored just 10 points, and for his first few games, focused a bit too much on passing the ball as opposed to scoring it for himself. Coach Prosser told Paul that if he continued to play that way, the opposing team would just stop guarding him. So Paul made it a point to score, and on December 2, 2003, he delivered. Against Indiana in the ACC-Big Ten Challenge, Paul had 20 points on just nine shots and also managed to produce eight assists and five steals in a blowout victory. Buoyed by Paul's effort, Wake Forest thrashed Indiana 100-67, the largest margin of victory in the Challenge's history. Indiana coach Mike Davis declared that Paul "may be the best point guard we have played against since I was in Indiana."

Paul may have been the best player for Wake Forest, but he was not their leading scorer. That was Justin Gray, a sharp-shooting guard who started alongside Paul. Paul and Gray formed a blazing guard combination that was hard to defend, and Wake Forest shot right out of the gate to start Paul's maiden college season. The Demon Deacons won their first 11 games but then struggled for the remainder of the season. They dropped several close games down the stretch and finished with a very respectable 21-10 record. Even though the team struggled at the end, Paul continued to play well. In a triple-overtime victory over the North Carolina Tar Heels, he played 46 minutes and finished with 18 points, eight assists, and five steals. Against the #12 Cincinnati Bearcats, Paul scored 30 points on 10 of 14 shooting, and also had a career-high seven rebounds. He did not miss his first shot until midway through the second half, and even then, he managed to score the putback.

Paul had performed extremely well in college basketball's regular season, and in the tournaments, he went to a whole different level. In the ACC tournament against Maryland, Paul did everything he could to lead Wake Forest to victory. He scored 30 points, including 5 points in the final minute of play despite leg cramps. It proved to not be enough. Maryland prevailed 87-86 on a last-second free throw. Even though Wake Forest had been knocked out of the ACC tournament in their first game, Chris Paul was still nominated to the Second Team All-ACC Tournament.

In the NCAA tournament, Wake Forest needed everything it could get from Paul as well. Paul scored 51 total points in the first two rounds against Virginia Commonwealth and Manhattan, games that Wake Forest won by a total of 5 points. Against Manhattan, he also had eight rebounds and six assists with just one turnover. Wake Forest then played Saint Joseph's in the regional semifinals. Saint Joseph's was led by their star, future NBA All-Star Jameer Nelson. Against Nelson, Paul's play dropped off, as he scored just 12 points and also had three turnovers. Saint Joseph's narrowly won, 84-80, as Nelson and fellow future NBA guard Delonte West each had 24 points.

Paul was disappointed with his play at the end of the NCAA tournament, and he called Coach Prosser to promise that he would improve. But his overall play in his freshmen year remained impressive. He averaged 14.8 points and 5.9 assists for the Demon Deacons, all while shooting almost 50% from the field and 46.5% from three-point range, the fourth highest three-point percentage in Wake Forest history. The awards came pouring in, too. Paul received the ACC Rookie of the Year award, was nominated to the All-ACC Third Team and the All-ACC Defensive team, and was named the National Freshman of the Year by College Insider, The Sporting News, Basketball Times, and Dick Vitale. Chris Paul decided to play at least one more year for Wake before trying his hand at the NBA Draft.

Sophomore Year

With another year of development, Wake Forest was expected to be one of the best college teams in the nation. Under Chris Paul's leadership, the Demon Deacons were happy to meet those expectations. They started strong, winning 15 of their first

16 games. Paul was once again happy to let Justin Gray and center Eric Williams lead the team in scoring, but there was no doubt that he was the team's leader. Though Paul played on a team without any other future NBA players, he still elevated his own game and that of his team's. In a January 15 victory against North Carolina, Paul had 26 points along with eight assists, six rebounds, and five steals. On February 12, Paul handed out seven assists in just 24 minutes of action as Wake Forest destroyed the Florida State Seminoles, 87-48. Florida State coach Leonard Hamilton called him a child prodigy, observing, "I'm not sure I have ever seen that kind of poise from a player at such a young age."

Unfortunately, even such a poised player could lose his cool at times. In the last game of the regular season against the North Carolina State Wolfpack, Paul punched opposing guard Julius Hodge in the groin, which sent Hodge straight to the ground. Paul hit a buzzer-beating runner to win the game, but the punch marred the victory. Paul apologized for his actions, but he was still suspended for one game. The game he was to miss happened to be Wake Forest's first game in the ACC tournament, which was a rematch against North Carolina State. Wake Forest was dazed and confused without their floor leader, and North Carolina State throttled the Demon Deacons 81-65. Julius Hodge led the Wolfpack with 22 points.

Paul hoped to get over losing in the first round of the ACC tournament again by leading Wake Forest to a March Madness victory, but he was again frustrated. After quickly dispatching Chattanooga in the first round, Wake Forest just could not contain West Virginia's offense in the second round. The match was a thrilling battle that lasted two overtimes, but West Virginia upset Wake Forest 111-105. Chris Paul had 22 points and nine assists, but he also had five turnovers in the game.

Even though Wake Forest had failed to win either in the ACC or NCAA in Paul's two years, he felt that he had nothing more to prove upon and thought that he could not have improved his game against collegiate-level basketball. Paul's numbers in his sophomore year barely improved from his freshman year, averaging 15.3 points and 6.6 assists. He was nominated to the First-Team Consensus All-American and was one of the top prospects in the NBA Draft. After pondering his next move, Paul made the decision to enter the NBA Draft. He had been one of the best players in Wake Forest's history, leading them to wins with his leadership and basketball skills. On March 3, 2013, Wake Forest retired Chris Paul's #3 jersey to a roaring crowd.

Chapter 4: Chris' NBA Career

Getting Drafted

The 2005 NBA Draft was not the best of draft classes compared to those that preceded it, especially the 2003 Draft class. However, three of the top 10 choices of the 2005 class, namely Paul, Deron Williams, and Andrew Bynum, were able to become All-Star players. And overall, five players from the class were able to become All-Stars at least once. It was a talented draft class indeed, but a lot of the lottery picks could not develop into game-changing players. Was Paul seen as one of those players?

Coming into the 2005 NBA Draft, Chris Paul was one of the best point guard prospects. There were three point guards in the draft class slated to be lottery picks, namely CP3, Williams, and Raymond Felton. People thought that nobody could go wrong by choosing one of those players over the other two. But Chris would prove to them later in his career that he was the best. Often compared to Hall of Fame point guard and NBA champion Isiah Thomas, Chris Paul had big shoes to fill. Both Thomas and Paul played the game as small point guards. Though their size was often seen as their weakness, both Chris and Isiah were always two of the most competitive and tough-minded point guards in NBA history. Moreover, Paul always had the same kind of leadership and ability to set the offense that Thomas had in his career with the Pistons.

Most scouts at that time would describe CP3 as a pure point guard. If you wanted to define a pure NBA point guard, there was no other player to look at than Chris Paul. With his maturity and gritty style of playing the position, Paul had all the makings of being the team leader at the point. He always made it a point to do the right things to improve the team's level of play. Chris made sure that he involved his teammates in any way possible with his ability to see the floor and make the toughest passes.

Though Chris Paul was strictly described as a pure passing point guard, he was always a good scorer despite his size. He had the ability to get into the paint and finish through contact as a 6-foot tall point guard. Paul had that ability because he had a quick first step and an explosiveness not usually seen from people his size. Almost nobody could stop him from getting to the basket if he wanted to even though he was pint-sized compared to the other slashing guards in the draft class. And despite his size, Paul has the innate ability to elude shot-blockers at the basket by knowing when to put up a shot quickly before defenders could react.

Most of Paul's drives to the basket and inside scoring came from pick-and-roll situations. That meant that Paul was a superb pick-and-roll player who could either look to pass to the rolling big man or take the ball to the basket with his explosive first step. Breaking down defenses was always Paul's specialty, and it was a skill needed of a point guard if he wanted his to get his teammates open looks.[iii]

In line with Chris Paul's ability to break down defenses, he is also skilled in knowing when to take advantage of weak defensive schemes. On the fast break, Paul knows when and how to get by defenses. In half-court situations, he understands how to take advantage of slacking rotations to get to the basket or looks for open teammates for easy baskets. And on isolation plays, Chris Paul is a master at splitting defenses and of leaving defenders behind with his ability to change his pace.

Concerning speed and quickness, Chris Paul is certainly as quick as any other speedy point guard in the draft class. Consider guys like TJ Ford and Raymond Felton, who were both quick in their rights. However, what got Paul miles ahead of those players was his ability to break defenses down not just with his speed and quickness, but also with his understanding of how they reacted in certain situations.

Shooting-wise, Chris Paul was never the best of shooters on the prep level or at the collegiate stage. But he grew into a safe and efficient shooter in his two years with Wake Forest. In his sophomore year, Paul hit 47 percent from the amateur three-point line. Though the NBA three-point arc is a lot farther than at the collegiate level, you can still say that Paul's shooting touch was already present, but could still use a little more refining in the professional league. He could also hit the pull-up jump shot, but he did not do so at a high rate. Offensively, Chris Paul was entering the NBA as a premier point guard who had the ability to become a floor leader, and at the same time, a scorer if needed.[iv]

Though Chris Paul did not have the creativity at making plays for other teammates like Magic Johnson, Steve Nash, and Jason Kidd, he certainly knew how to run an offensive effectively minus the flair of all-time great point guards before him. In Wake Forest, he had an incredibly high assist-to-turnover ratio because of his efficiency at handling the ball and making timely passes. And though you might not see the magic of an Earvin Johnson in the way he makes plays, Paul understands tempo and how to react to broken plays just as well as Magic did.

On the other end of the court, CP3 never let his opponent get the best of him. Paul was always a short point guard, but he could stay with his man using his speed and lateral quickness. Having a low center of gravity and a powerful body meant that Chris was not an easy defender to push around and get physical with. His basketball awareness is so high that it extends all the way to the defensive part of the floor, and it gives him the ability to read the opposing team's offense. Because of that IQ and his quick hands, Chris Paul tends to get a lot of steals off his man or through interceptions.[v]

As good a point guard prospect as Chris was in the 2005 Draft, he still had some chinks in his armor. His height may have given him his competitive attitude, but it was still a weakness nonetheless, especially when matched up with taller guards at the NBA level. His lack of height could also hinder him from seeing over the top of defenders to make plays for other people.

And while Chris Paul always had that competitive edge in him, he lacked a certain kind of aggression needed from scoring point guards. Paul had an impressive array of offensive tools while he was in college. Despite having them, Chris only averaged about 15 points in his two years in college. What that could have implied was that he lacked aggression in getting his points, and he always made it a point to distribute the ball. As we all know, point guards are meant to make plays for other teammates. But with the offensive capabilities that Chris Paul had, one would wonder why he never scored as much as he could despite being able to score better than his teammates.

On defense, Chris Paul also lacked the same kind of aggression he lacked on offense. At barely 6 feet tall, Paul should have been more aggressive in defending his man because it was the only way for him to make up for his size on the defensive end of the floor. He always had the lateral quickness and low base to be able to defend at a high level, but Paul never actually made it a point every game to defend his man with grit and aggression. Chris also had a tendency of trying to get steals at every play possible. That tendency often translated into broken defensive plays. Finally, Chris Paul's competitiveness might have been a little too much for the NBA level. CP3 could get so competitive and hotheaded on the court that he forgot his importance to the team as its leader.[vi] Nevertheless, any team needs a certain level of competitiveness, ala Michael Jordan and Kobe Bryant. But a little too much of it could throw the team into disarray.

Overall, Chris Paul was entering the league as a bonafide point guard who could immediately make an impact with his ability to set up people and with his offensive skill set. He was always a competitive man, and unsuccessful teams need a lot of competitive spunk to play toe-to-toe with the best teams in the NBA. But size was always an issue with him, and it harmed his stock, especially when matched up against bigger opponents. And it sure did, since all the players that were chosen ahead of Paul were bigger guys.

As good of a player as Paul was, the Milwaukee Bucks could not pass up the opportunity to draft the best big man prospect. They selected Australian center Andrew Bogut with the first pick in the 2005 NBA draft. Second, the Atlanta Hawks picked North Carolina freshman and standout high school wingman Marvin Williams. Then the Utah Jazz opted to go with a bigger and more mature point guard in Illinois junior Deron Williams with the third pick.

Many people thought the Jazz chose the right point guard because Williams is a lot bigger than Paul is. Deron was slated to be a favorite for the Rookie of the Year award. With the consensus top draft pick already taken and with one of the three best point guards in the draft class already unavailable, the New Orleans Hornets finally grabbed Paul with the fourth pick. Chris Paul officially became an NBA player and was seen as an instant starter, especially since the Hornets, a team nowhere near playoff contention, were lacking a playmaker that could hopefully make the team competitive.

Rookie Season

The New Orleans Hornets were historically never a very a good NBA team, even back when the team was still playing in Charlotte. They were never good enough to be real playoff contenders despite having been able to reach the playoffs when the team was still in the Eastern Conference. Even when the team was still known as the Charlotte Hornets and with players such as Alonzo Mourning and Glen Rice, they could never get over the hump.

In 1996, they had the chance to flip history when they drafted an 18-year old Kobe Bryant, a player full of potential who was destined to become one of the best players in NBA history. However, they opted to trade the 13th-pick youngster to the Los Angeles Lakers in exchange for an aging Vlade Divac. The franchise could have been so much better had they kept Kobe. But heading into the 2005-06 season, the New Orleans Hornets were optimistic, especially because they were able to grab such a talented point guard as Chris Paul. Paul marked the beginning of a fresh new era for the New Orleans franchise.

The Hornets were more than willing to build around Chris Paul, but as his rookie season began, they had practically nothing aside from Paul himself. Coach Byron Scott had made the NBA

Finals twice back in 2002 and 2003 as the coach of the New Jersey Nets, but the Hornets had traded their best player, former All-Star center Jamaal Magloire, right before the season began. A bunch of middling veterans and youngsters like David West, P.J. Brown, and Desmond Mason were some of the key pieces on the Hornets. And since the only other point guard near Paul's level was the smaller Speedy Claxton, Paul was made an immediate starter for the Hornets. If the roster was not bad enough, the New Orleans Hornets were not even playing in New Orleans. The city was in no condition to host NBA games in the aftermath of the devastation of Hurricane Katrina, and the Hornets were forced to relocate to Oklahoma City.

The Hornets braced themselves for yet another miserable season, not just because of their line-up, but also because of the damage left by Hurricane Katrina. But Chris Paul would have none of it and immediately brought the same maturity and poise that he had shown in college at Wake Forest. The rest of the Hornets rallied around their new leader and picked up from his lead. David West blossomed into an excellent mid-range jump shooting power forward as well as a good option at the post, and Byron Scott got the Hornets to play hard defense. Chris Paul brought stability to the Hornets' offense despite playing in only his first year as a professional player. New Orleans seemed nothing like the team they were the previous year because they had CP3 handling the quarterback duties.

In his first game as an NBA player, Chris Paul scored 13 points, grabbed eight rebounds, and dished out four assists in a blowout win against the Sacramento Kings. His breakout game was when he scored 26 points on 10 out of 14 shooting from the field against the Dallas Mavericks in a loss. Three days later on November 15, 2005, he would have his first double-double game of points and assists as he finished a loss to the Miami Heat with 16 points and ten assists. Chris Paul would start out his NBA career scoring in double digits during his first nine outings. His highlight performance in that stretch was on November 18 when he had 25 points, 12 assists, and five steals in a win over the Atlanta Hawks.

Early in the season, it seemed as if Chris Paul had already begun to defy expectations. Everyone knew that he was a capable player coming into the NBA, but nobody thought he was going to be an immediate impact player for a struggling Hornets franchise. Throughout his first 27 games in his rookie season, CP3 was already showing signs of his scoring brilliance, putting up double-digit scoring numbers in 25 of those outings. He also had eight double-double performances including a near triple-double game of 17 points, 12 rebounds, and nine assists against the San Antonio Spurs on December 18.

As the season unfolded, Chris Paul was proving that his strong start was not a fluke as he continued to get better and better every month. On January 20, 2006, Paul had a then career-best 28 points to go along with 11 assists in a loss to the Washington Wizards. Then, in his first visit to New York as an NBA player just a day after, he had 27 points, 13 assists, and seven rebounds in a big win for the New Orleans Hornets.

Early in February, Chris Paul was further cementing himself as a premiere playmaker when he dished out 13 assists a night in three straight games. He would then represent and headline the freshmen players in the All-Star Rookie Challenge held in the middle of that month. At that point in that, there was already no doubt that CP3 was the favorite to win the Rookie of the Year award.

Chris Paul was also showing how great of an all-around player he was despite his size. While his scoring and passing skills were already earning him high praises, it was his rebounding at 6-feet tall that was even more impressive. CP3 would have his first career triple-double on April 2 in a win over the Toronto Raptors. He finished with 24 points, 12 rebounds, and 12 assists.

Three days later, he had 17 points, 11 rebounds, and 16 assists for his second career triple-double. But despite all of his brilliance as a freshman, Chris Paul alone could not carry the Hornets back to relevance that season.

Nevertheless, Paul was there to lead the Hornets down the stretch, and his consistent, solid play was reciprocated by winning the Western Conference Rookie of the Month award from start to finish. Chris Paul seemed as if he was playing beyond his years and was outplaying other point guards who had been in the NBA for several years already. He was undoubtedly the best rookie that year, having led the young crop in points, assists, and steals. He was even the league leader for total steals.

Chris Paul averaged 16.1 points, 7.8 assists, and 5.1 rebounds per game, and became the hands-down choice for the Rookie of the Year award, garnering 124 of the 125 first-place votes. He would have been a unanimous winner of that award had in not been for a single first place vote that was given to Deron Williams. Despite Chris Paul's success and immediate impact, the Hornets did have another losing season, but they finished 38-44, far better than anyone had predicted at the beginning of the 2005-06 season, and they were obviously far better than they had been the last two seasons.

Sophomore Year

New Orleans acquired two veteran impact role players through offseason trades. Those players would prove to be what the Hornets needed as their rising point guard continued to improve. First, the team acquired 7'1" center Tyson Chandler from the Chicago Bulls by shipping out J.R. Smith and P.J. Brown. Chandler was a good starting center for any team because of his length, defensive presence, and rebounding prowess. Though he was very limited offensively, he made shots when they mattered most.

Their second offseason acquisition was a veteran and former All-Star wingman Peja Stojakovic. Peja was a former high-volume scorer for the Kings and made his money by hitting outside shots. He provided much-needed wing scoring for the Hornets, who lacked a lot in that department. The team also acquired Bobby Jackson, who played alongside Stojakovic in Sacramento's best seasons. Jackson was regarded as the best backup point guard in the NBA for many years. A veteran like him could act as a mentor to a younger point guard like CP3.

The Hornets were still stuck in Oklahoma City during the 2006-07 season, though they began to play home games in New Orleans now and then as the city continued to rehabilitate from the devastation left by Katrina. But the Oklahoma crowd was very welcoming to the Hornets, and they breathed new life into the team's home games. Paul and his new teammates looked to rally to the roar of the OKC fandom and were poised to make some noise in the NBA.

In Paul's fifth game of the season, he scored above 30 points for the first time in his career with a 34-point performance against Golden State. He also finished that game with ten assists for a double-double performance. Chris Paul had four double-doubles in the first five games of the season. Nine days later, he scored 35 points against the Minnesota Timberwolves. He would then have his third career triple-double and a new career high in assists when he finished with 25 points, 11 rebounds, and 18 assists in a loss to the Chicago Bulls on December 1, 2006.

But while the Hornets had hoped to improve with the new acquisitions of defensive center Tyson Chandler and sharpshooter Peja Stojakovic, the problems of trying to become contenders in a tough conference was still too much for New Orleans, especially since their core was still young. On top of that, Paul missed 17 games in December and January due to injuries. Stojakovic would also play only 13 games for the whole season because of a nagging back injury. In addition to dooming New Orleans's hopes of making the playoffs, the injuries also prevented Paul from making his first ever All-Star game appearance.

Paul would, however, play in the 2007 All-Star Weekend Rookie Challenge, where he broke the single-game records for both assists and steals with 17 and 9, respectively. His sights were set on the Saturday midseason classic. Paul vowed to make the All-Star game next season and managed to improve his averages to 17.3 points and 8.9 assists per game. It was evident that CP3 was quickly rising through the ranks as one of the best point guards in the NBA and could very well become the best in a few years. Thanks to Chandler, veteran teammates Desmond Mason and Bobby Jackson, and the improvement of guys like Devin Brown and Rasual Butler, the Hornets managed to improve to 39 wins despite Paul's and Peja's injuries, but the team was determined to make the postseason the following season.

Rise to All-Star Status, Contending for the MVP

The Hornets returned to the city of New Orleans full-time since the damage left by Hurricane Katrina was all but gone as far as basketball operations were concerned. The Hornets were poised to become playoff contenders as they built upon the significant improvements from the previous season, especially with how fast West and Paul were improving and with a healthy Stojakovic and Chandler playing off of their best duo.

Many sports analysts expected New Orleans to make the playoffs in the 2007-08 season, but as a lower seed that would be promptly dispatched in the first round by one of the top teams like Phoenix or San Antonio. But just like in his rookie year, Chris Paul proceeded to surpass everyone's expectations completely.

In their full-season return to New Orleans that year, the Hornets put on a show for their long-suffering fans. Tyson Chandler and Byron Scott managed the defense, David West scored in the post, and Peja Stojakovic lurked with a deadly 3-point shot. But Chris Paul was always the centerpiece. He was the one who made everyone else look good. Tyson was the defensive anchor, but he did not have any post moves. With Paul breaking down the defense, Chandler was able to find good open looks inside the paint. He was also CP3's best option for the lob pass, and the big guy delivered all the time with rim-rattling alley-oop dunks.

For Peja's part, he was already getting older and could no longer score at will compared to his Sacramento years. But Paul made life easier for him. Peja found open spots on the court for perimeter and three-point shots because his point guard did his best in finding him. West became Chris Paul's partner off the pick-and-roll/pop situations. He was also the best option at the low post for New Orleans. With Paul leading, everything went well for the surging Hornets.

Running the show for the New Orleans Hornets was what Chris Paul had to do night in and night out that season. He did it to perfection and he made life easier for Coach Byron Scott and his capable teammates. The Hornets ran off to a 4-0 start that season capped off by Paul's 19 points and then career-high 21 assists in a win over the Los Angeles Lakers.

On December 7, 2007, against the Memphis Grizzlies, Paul played 49 minutes in an overtime game and scored a new career-high 43 points. It was not the only highlight performance CP3 would have that season as he continued to fill the stats sheet with his all-around effort in scoring, rebounding, and assisting. On top of that, he was still able to play the elite level defense he was known for, while virtually doing everything else for his team.

Chris Paul would have his second career 40-point game on December 26 as he scored 40 points on 17 out of 25 shooting from the field in only 36 minutes of action in a win over the

Memphis Grizzlies once again. But while putting up terrific stats was what Paul was accustomed to doing ever since his rookie season, what made his performances even more special this season was that he was winning games for his climbing team.

From early January up to February, Chris Paul had 11 straight games of putting up double-digit assists. It was capped off by a 19-assist game in a loss to the Kings on February 1, 2008. Chris Paul was the primary catalyst of a nine-game winning streak for his Hornets in that stretch of impressive performances on the passing end.

On February 6, Paul dueled with Phoenix's two-time MVP point guard Steve Nash in a match that lasted two overtimes. Paul picked Nash's pocket repeatedly, forcing him into ten turnovers while he grabbed eight steals. He also had 42 points as the Hornets won 132-130. Chris Paul outplayed the two-time MVP and the player regarded as the best point guard at that time. Paul finished with 42 points, nine assists, and eight steals while Nash had 32 points and 12 assists.

Paul's consistent performances throughout the season made people turn their eyes towards the rising point guard. Not only was Paul playing like a phenom, but his team was also a playoff contender fighting for one of the top spots in the West against teams like the Spurs and Lakers. And with the way he was playing all facets of the game at a high level for an undersized point guard, Chris Paul was quickly dethroning guys like Steve Nash and Jason Kidd for the mantle of the best point guard in the world at that time. With his elevated play and the success his team found, CP3 became an All-Star for the first time in his career.

In the 2008 All-Star game held in New Orleans, Paul, alongside David West, was nominated for his first All-Star game. CP3 played very well for a first-timer in the midseason classic. He scored 16 points and dished out a game-high 14 assists as well as pilfering the ball four times. Chris Paul was a serious contender for the All-Star MVP award, especially with how he helped the West crawl out from a fourth-quarter deficit to make the game tight. But the Western All-Stars eventually lost the game, and LeBron James became the game's Most Valuable Player. Had the West won, Paul might have been the best player among his fellow All-Stars.

As the season continued to unfold, the Hornets constantly battled with the Lakers for the top seed in the West. And with the two teams battling for Western Conference supremacy, their best players were also going toe-to-toe for the most coveted individual award in the NBA—the Most Valuable Player award. Chris Paul and Kobe Bryant continued to trade places atop the MVP ladder as the Hornets and Lakers also traded places day after day atop the West. In the end, the Lakers edged out the Hornets in a game that seemed to decide the winner of the first seed. In the Hornet's fourth-to-final game of the regular season, they lost a close game to the Lakers, 104 to 107. New Orleans would only win one game after that, and the Lakers solidified their position atop the West.

Nevertheless, the Hornets finished with 56 victories, the second-best record in the Western Conference, and won the Southwest Division title for the first time in franchise history. Their 56 wins were the best that the franchise had ever gotten, and it was all thanks to the MVP-like play of their star point guard. It was likewise a banner season for Chris Paul, who did not just make the All-Star game, but also finished second in MVP voting to the Lakers' superstar guard Kobe Bryant.

It seemed that Paul and Kobe's duel in the Hornets' 79th regular season game not only had playoff seeding implications, but it also decided which player was the rightful MVP. In the end, Kobe edged Paul out not only that game, but in the coveted award voting as well. Kobe finished with 1,105 voting points while Chris Paul was second with 889 voting points and 28 first place votes. Had the Hornets won the first seed, CP3 would have been the MVP of the season. To this day, many analysts and fans believe that Paul should have won the award that year.

Chris Paul was also named to the All-NBA First Team as well as the NBA All-Defensive Second Team. Over the regular season, he averaged 21.1 points on 48.8% shooting, an incredible percentage for a point guard. He also led the league with 11.6 assists and 2.7 steals per game. With his numbers and with how well he managed to win games with the Hornets, Chris Paul was quickly becoming the best point guard in the NBA if he was not already the best at that point in his career. Not even Steve Nash or Jason Kidd could duplicate the numbers that Paul was putting up that season.

The 2008 NBA playoffs began and New Orleans faced off against the Dallas Mavericks in the first round. The Hornets had not won a playoff series since 2002, back when they were still located in Charlotte. Dallas had traded for the future Hall of Fame point guard Jason Kidd to improve their chances of winning a title that season. But while Devin Harris, the player whom Dallas traded for Kidd, had the length and athleticism needed to defend Chris Paul, the 35-year old Jason Kidd, who had already lost a lot of quickness over the years, did not.

In Game 1, Dallas raced out to the early lead, 52-40 at the half. Paul had 11 points, but the ESPN halftime crew noted that he needed to take over if the Hornets were to win. Paul did precisely that. He scored 24 points in the second half and led the Hornets to the 104-92 victory. He had 35 points and ten assists for the game, one of the most impressive playoff debuts in NBA history.

In Game 2, Paul set a team playoff record with 17 assists. He again led the team from start to finish as the Hornets won every quarter against the Mavs. At the end of the game, New Orleans won by 24 in a 127-103 blowout victory. Paul was spectacular once again. Along with his 17 assists, he also scored 32 points. His output in Games 1 and 2 became the best two-game playoff debut for any player in NBA history. Paul scored more than 30 per game and assisted on a total of 27 baskets in his first two postseason appearances.

While the Mavs were able to get a win in Game 3 on the strength of a monster performance by their very own superstar, Dirk Nowitzki, who had 32 points and 19 rebounds, the Hornets quickly bounced back in Game 4 with David West scoring 30 points. It seemed like the Hornets were too good and like they had the Mavs' numbers for that first-round meeting. The Hornets proved that by beating Dallas back in New Orleans, 99 to 94. David West was again terrific in that game with 29 points. Meanwhile, Paul assisted on 15 baskets. New Orleans went on to defeat Dallas in 5 games where Paul averaged 24.6 points, 12 assists, and 5.6 rebounds. In the series-clinching Game 5, he had a triple-double of 24 points, 15 assists, and 11 rebounds. That was his first playoff triple-double.

In the second round, Chris Paul faced off against fellow Wake Forest alumnus Tim Duncan and the San Antonio Spurs. The Spurs had an elite point guard in 2007 Finals MVP Tony Parker. Parker was just as quick and savvy as Chris Paul was. But the biggest advantage that Parker had over Paul was his extensive experience and championship pedigree. While Parker really could not defend Paul because he was not an elite defender, Parker's quickness meant that he could score right back and could make life just as difficult for CP3.

By using home court advantage, the Hornets immediately pounced on a Spurs team that was deemed as too old for the younger New Orleans squad. It was an all-around team effort for the Hornets. West and Stojakovic handled the scoring duties while Chandler rebounded the ball and limited the legendary Tim Duncan to only 5 points. But Paul was the difference-maker in Game 1 with his double-double effort of 17 points and 13 assists to go along with four steals. New Orleans blew San

Antonio out of the Smoothie King Center by a score of 101 to 82.

Game 2 was not very different from Game 1. Again, Paul was the catalyst on both ends of the floor. While Duncan found resurgence in Game 2 as he was keeping Chandler in foul trouble, Paul just did not care. He scored 30 points on an efficient 11 out of 20 from the field. He also assisted on 12 baskets, including on several outside shots for Peja Stojakovic, who had 25 in the game. Paul also had three steals in his matchup with the reigning Finals MVP Tony Parker.

The Hornets won the first two games of the series and had the defending champions on their heels. But as the scene shifted back to San Antonio, the Spurs regained the momentum, especially because of their veteran smarts and championship experience. In Game 3, Paul scored 35 points, including an incredible circus shot where he threw the ball behind his head and into the basket, but Parker answered with 31 points of his own as the Spurs won 110-99. Ginobili also scored 31 as a starter. For New Orleans, only their All-Star duo performed well in game 3.

In game 4, the Spurs were intent on allowing Paul to take over the scoring load, but did not allow him to get his teammates involved. The Hornets' catalyst, Chris Paul was limited to only five assists, his lowest yet for the playoffs that year, even as he scored 23 points. Only two other Hornets were in double-digit scoring. Meanwhile, the Spurs' Big Three managed to score a total of 58 combined points to rout New Orleans 100 to 80. By losing game 4, the Hornets were tied 2-2 with the Spurs, and the series became a virtual best-of-three series.

It seemed as if both teams were going to defend their home floors to the last of their breath by winning all home games. Game 5 was no different. Back in New Orleans, the Hornets relied on the dominant play of their All-Star power forward to win their third blowout victory over the Spurs in the series. West had 38 big points, and Paul recorded a double-double with 22 points and 14 assists. The Spurs would win their own home game by 19 points. They again limited the rest of the Hornets not named Chris Paul to tie the series 3-3 and send it to a deciding game 7.

The home team had won all of the first six games. Moreover, all the wins by either team were in double digits. It seemed that by having home court advantage, the Hornets were on their way to the Conference Finals if the trend continued. But in the deciding Game 7 in New Orleans, Paul was limited to just 18 points. He still had 14 assists and limited Parker to 17 points. But the Spurs had too much championship and veteran experience in their lineup, and they also had Manu Ginobili and Duncan alongside Parker, while the Hornets revolved almost entirely around Paul. Manu scored 26 and Duncan lorded over the boards with 14. San Antonio won 91-82, and New Orleans's Cinderella season came to an end with their failure to slay the defending champions. The Spurs would later lose to the eventual finalists, the Los Angeles Lakers. In Paul's playoff debut, he averaged an incredible stat line of 24.1 points, 11.3 assists, 4.9 rebounds, and 2.3 steals.

Being the Best Point Guard in the NBA

After re-signing with the Hornets for $68 million, Chris Paul entered the 2008-09 season determined to replicate the previous year's success and reach the NBA Finals, especially with the core lineup intact and ready to make more noise. The New Orleans Hornets, banking on having their core players do what they do best, did not do much in the offseason other than extending Paul's contract and signing defensive wingman James Posey fresh from an NBA championship run with the Celtics. With that, the Hornets still had enough talent and experience to become top Western Conference contenders.

Naturally, it was Chris Paul keeping the boat floating for the New Orleans Hornets in that early stretch of the season. He started the 2008-09 season posting seven straight games of at least 20 points and ten assists. CP3 left off where he started in the 2007-08 season when he was almost the Most Valuable Player in the NBA. Chris Paul would even record two consecutive triple-doubles as he gave his Hornets a 7-5 start for the year.

But things took a different turn. Tyson Chandler and Peja Stojakovic were never the healthiest NBA players, but the two of them had missed just eight total games back in 2007-08. This stroke of luck did not last. Stojakovic missed 21 games, and Chandler missed 37 games due to continued feet issues. Without Stojakovic's shooting and Chandler's ability to defend and finish at the rim, the Hornets suffered. Despite those key injuries, Paul played his heart out and led the team. He and David West played more than 38 minutes per game to negate the roster's injury problems the team faced throughout the season. Paul set the NBA record for most consecutive games with a steal at 106 games on December 17 and continued to solidify his name as the best ball thief in the NBA. Against the Philadelphia 76ers on January 26, 2009, he nearly had a quadruple double with 27 points, 15 assists, ten rebounds, and seven steals.

Even as the Hornets struggled to get to the level they were at in the 2007-08 season, Paul and David West made the All-Star team. Chris Paul played very well in the All-Star game as per usual. He had 14 points, 14 assists, and three steals for the winning Western Conference All-Stars. Despite another stellar performance, the All-Star MVP was awarded to the legendary duo of Kobe Bryant and Shaquille O'Neal, who reunited as teammates for one last game.

Chris Paul would never waver as the season progressed past the All-Star break. Showing that he was indeed an unselfish superstar, CP3 recorded 20 dimes in a win over the Milwaukee Bucks on February 27, 2009, even though he scored only 19 points himself. Barely two weeks later, he would record his sixth and final triple-double of the season as he showed the world that his size was never a factor in his ability to play all facets of the game at elite levels.

Near the end of the regular season, Chris Paul turned in two of his best individual scoring performances. He first scored 43 points against the Golden State Warriors on April 3, 2009, when he made 16 of his 28 field goal attempts. CP3 then scored 42 points against the Dallas Mavericks just a week later. He made 14 of his 25 shots in that game. However, both performances came at losses for a New Orleans Hornets team that could not replicate the same kind of magic they had during the previous season.

At the end of the season, Paul was still good enough to make the All-NBA Second Team. He could have been a First Team member had it not been for the MVP-like year that Dwyane Wade had. Paul was then elevated as a member of the All-Defensive First Team. He averaged 22.8 points on over 50% shooting as well as 11 assists and 2.8 steals per game. His assists and steals numbers were, for the second straight season, the top in the NBA.

Paul also achieved a 29.96 PER, the highest PER in an NBA season by a point guard. At that point of his career, there was no doubt in anyone's mind that Chris Paul was the best point guard in the NBA, especially since Steve Nash and Jason Kidd were already moving past their prime.

But Paul would soon be challenged at that spot in later years as then rookies Derrick Rose and Russell Westbrook were climbing the point guard ranks as quickly as their feet could run the floor. Young and talented point guards like Stephen Curry were also ready to show their quality in the NBA. And of course, Tony Parker was still around to prove that there was more than one elite point guard in the league.

Despite these incredible statistical achievements, there was only so much Paul could do to handle the lack of help around him. The Hornets dropped to 49 wins as the seventh seed in the West. While they made the NBA Playoffs again, they were up against the Denver Nuggets in the first round. This time, it was their turn to be the underdogs, especially since they were the lower-seeded team. Meanwhile, Denver was having one of their best NBA seasons with the leadership of Chauncey Billups and the high-volume scoring of Carmelo Anthony.

The Nuggets brought the fight to the New Orleans Hornets the moment the opening tip was tossed. Though Chris Paul remained as a consistent 20-10 guy on offense, the veteran big shot maker Chauncey Billups, who scored 36 points, outplayed him. The Nuggets went on to win the game 113 to 84 on the strength of their bench players. Meanwhile, no Hornets bench player was in double-digit scoring.

Game 2 was more of the same. Billups again outplayed Chris Paul in their point guard duel. Paul had another double-double, but only scored 14 points and assisted on 13 baskets. On the other end, the bigger and much more experienced Chauncey drilled bucket after bucket for 31 points. Billups was so good in the first two games that the Nuggets did not notice that their leading scorer Carmelo Anthony was genuinely struggling to start the playoffs. It did not matter, however, because the Hornets just could not get going. In the end, New Orleans fell to 0-2.

While his small frame was always what made him as competitive as he is, Chris Paul's lack of size proved to be his downfall in that matchup against Chauncey Billups. While Billups did not have the same talent and natural feel for the game that Paul had, he was bigger and more experienced. He used the full extent of his size and experience against a smaller and younger CP3.

Paul got his revenge over Billups in game 3. And he was also happy to get a win to close the series to 1-2. In a very close and physical battle, the Hornets managed to fend off the Nuggets on their home floor with a 95-93 victory. CP3 was the star of the game with 32 points and 12 assists after being outplayed by Chauncey Billups, who had 16, in the first two games. However, this was the closest they were to the Nuggets throughout the series.

Game 4 punctuated the disappointing end to the season when Denver annihilated New Orleans 121-63. It tied the most lopsided defeat in NBA playoff history, first achieved back in 1956. The New Orleans Hornets just could not score despite the Nuggets not being known for their defense. Paul probably had the worst playoff game of his life with only 4 points and six assists for the hapless Hornets. Though the Hornets could not score, Denver was doing so at will. Seven players, led by Carmelo Anthony, were in double-digit scoring.

Down 1-3 in the series, the New Orleans Hornets were too discouraged and disheartened to put up a gritty fight as the Nuggets finally ended their misery with another blowout win. Paul had another double-double with 12 and ten, but the Nuggets were just too good for them to handle. In the end, Paul's 2009 playoff run ended a lot quicker than his playoff debut the previous year.

Chris Paul averaged less-than-stellar numbers in his five-game playoff appearance with 16.6 points and 10.6 assists on 41% shooting. While those numbers would have been acceptable for any other point guard in the NBA, it was not what was expected from the best playmaker in the league. Whether the struggle was because of Billups' size or his lack of help on offense, it was clear that Chris Paul needed contribute to take his team to greater heights.

Injury Season

Stunned by the disaster against Denver, the Hornets decided to revamp the roster around Chris Paul for the 2009-10 season. Tyson Chandler, who was supposed to be traded over to the OKC Thunder the previous season, was traded for another defensive center in Emeka Okafor. They were also able to get younger pieces by drafting Darren Collison and Marcus Thornton, who would both have solid NBA careers.

Coach Byron Scott was fired after the Hornets lost 6 of their first nine games. Chris Paul was displeased with the sudden change. He stated that as the star player of the Hornets, he should have been informed in advance about the coaching change. Moreover, he loved Tyson Chandler as a teammate because he was his best option when he threw lob passes up top. Okafor, as good of a defender and post player as he was, just could not mesh well with Paul.

Nevertheless, CP3 tried his best to right the ship of the Hornets while also providing good solid numbers that were on par with his status as an elite player in the NBA. In New Orleans' second win of the season, Chris Paul scored 39 big points as he seemed to be the sole scorer of the Hornets in that outing. But as LeBron James pondered his future with the Cleveland Cavaliers, sports bloggers and analysts began to wonder about Chris Paul's long-term future with the New Orleans Hornets.

Unfortunately, Chris Paul soon faced a bigger issue. After missing eight games in November 2009, Paul looked to have another spectacular All-Star season. He came back to the lineup ready to wreak havoc once more. Though his offense was still out of tune, Paul never forgot to focus on making plays for his teammates. He had seven straight games of double-doubles on points and assists while never slacking on the defensive end. The Hornets were 5-2 in that stretch. Everything seemed right when the New Orleans Hornets, under CP3's leadership, started the year with six straight wins.

But on January 27, 2010, he injured his left knee against the Golden State Warriors. Paul brushed off the knee injury and continued to play that game. Given that he finished with 38 points, nine assists, and six rebounds in a victory over the Warriors, he seemed just fine. But in the next game against the Chicago Bulls, Paul went out of bounds to save a ball and collided into a sports camera. The impact tore the meniscus in his left knee, which is a grave injury that requires arthroscopic surgery.

While Paul had been nominated to the All-Star game for a third straight year, he was forced to miss the game, and his spot went to Chauncey Billups. Paul sat out for almost the entire season, only coming back for seven ineffectual games at the end. Rookie point guard Darren Collison filled in for him. While Collison was a draft steal for the Hornets and while he turned out to be a solid point guard, he was nowhere near Paul's level as a playmaker or scorer.

The New Orleans Hornets never made enough damage to become relevant in the NBA because of the injury that their star point guard had to recover from. Though Paul would make a return in March, it was all too little too late. Moreover, it also seemed like the superstar playmaker was not quite in top form at that point of the season as he struggled even to put up points on the board.

Without their star point guard, the Hornets missed the playoffs and finished with a 37-45 record, their worst since drafting Paul. Chris Paul finished the season averaging 18.7 points, 4.2 rebounds, 10.7 assists, and 2.1 steals while shooting his highest clip of 49.3% from the field. Though his numbers were still at an elite level, Paul's inability to stay healthy was what proved to be the downfall of his team. He would only play 45 games that season.

Frustration and Trade

Young former NBA player Monty Williams took over as head coach of the New Orleans Hornets for the 2010-11 season. The Hornets also made several roster changes. With Stojakovic aging and saddled by injuries, the team had to get another wing player to fill-in for the former All-Star. Darren Collison, who was deemed expendable with CP3 returning to full health, was traded along with James Posey to the Indiana Pacers in exchange for former champion small forward Trevor Ariza.

While Ariza was not a scorer like Peja, he was much younger then and a much better defender. The Hornets also acquired Italian shooter Marco Belinelli to replace Rasual Butler as their primary three-point threat. And with backup point guard Collison traded, they brought in Jarrett Jack. It was a whole new, different lineup from the team that had made the second round of the playoffs barely three seasons ago.

On Paul's part, many sports athletes never fully recover after knee surgeries, and for a time, there was a fear that Chris Paul would never be the same. While Paul did not quite manage to reach his 2008 MVP-level peak in the 2010-11 season, he remained one of the best point guards in the league. But the bigger and more athletic youngster Derrick Rose of the Chicago

Bulls challenged Paul's position atop the list of point guards. Rose solidified his name as the best point guard in the NBA by winning the MVP later in the season. Paul, meanwhile, could have been the better player had he not been rusty from injury.

Nevertheless, Chris Paul was still playing at an elite level despite struggling to get back to his peak form after the injury he had suffered a season prior. He started off the season leading the New Orleans Hornets to eight consecutive wins without losing a game. However, his numbers did not take off in that stretch, but he did just enough to act as the leader and primary catalyst. He had three double-doubles in those eight straight wins. His best performance was 13 points, 19 assists, and five steals in a win over the Miami Heat on November 5, 2010.

But everyone knew that the Hornets would just fold as the season progressed, especially because their best player still was not playing at his full capacity. Chris Paul, though still the best at running an offense, was not as potent on the offensive end as he had always been in the other four seasons he had played in the NBA. Paul's scoring numbers saw a dip. Nevertheless, no other player in the NBA could match his ability at making plays.

Most importantly, CP3's knee seemed to be just fine, and he played 80 games that season, although his scoring dropped to

15.9 points a game, the lowest of his career. He only scored above 30 points once in the regular season. He still managed to make the All-Star game as well as the All-NBA Third Team. Paul, West, and Okafor combined to create an offensive and defensive core, and the New Orleans Hornets won 46 games and returned to the playoffs. Monty Williams turned the roster into a defense-oriented team. They lost David West to a season-ending injury but midseason acquisition Carl Landry was up to the task as the starting power forward.

New Orleans faced two-time defending champions the Los Angeles Lakers in the first round. While the Lakers were still a fantastic team that season, their superstar Kobe Bryant was playing injured, and the team faced other issues that hindered them from playing their best. Despite that, they were still the defending champs and had enough in them to make a run for another three-peat.

Chris Paul's return to the playoffs was a fantastic one. He scored 33 points against the Lakers in Game 1, including 9 in the last two minutes of play, to shock the Lakers in a 109-100 win. Paul also had 14 assists. Meanwhile, Kobe Bryant matched Paul's output with 34 points. In Game 2, Paul continued to play well with 20 points and nine rebounds but was playing without help other than Trevor Ariza's 22 points. The Hornets managed to score only 78 points despite playing good defense on the Lakers who scored only 87.

The Hornets went back home for Games 3 and 4. In their first game at home, it seemed like the All-Star trio of Bryant, Gasol, and Bynum was too much to handle as they fell again to the Lakers 86 to 100. Paul scored 22 points and had eight dimes, but was again missing help from his teammates. Paul had a triple-double of 27 points, 15 assists, and 13 rebounds in a bounce-back game 4 to power his team to victory and to tie the series 2-2.

Paul would get help from Belinelli and Ariza in Game 5, but the Lakers played a more balanced attack with six players in double-digit scoring to win the game by 16 points. Game 6 was more of the same. The Hornets had no other option aside from Paul, who only had 10 points but dished out 11 assists. Meanwhile, the Laker roster was full of offensive weapons that all made the New Orleans Hornets bow out of the playoffs.

While the Hornets won two games, the Lakers won the rest of the games, prevailing whenever Paul did not have a superhuman game. It was just another example of how a single player can only impact the court so much. In his first playoff season after recovering from injury, Chris Paul was a one-man show with 22 points per game, 11.5 assists a night, and 6.7 boards per outing. The only positive outcome that anyone could derive from that performance in the playoffs was that Chris Paul had seemingly returned to his elite form as a point guard.

Though Paul was still the leader of the Hornets and the best point guard in the NBA, he was not happy with how the New Orleans front office was handling the roster. Reports surfaced that he wanted out of NOLA as soon as his contract ended. With that, people anticipated that Hornets management might think to pursue a trade involving their star point guard out of fear that the franchise would not be able to get anything in return if Paul moved out of New Orleans via free agency.

That summer's offseason was the most tumultuous of Chris Paul's career. Paul had the option of becoming a free agent at the end of the 2011-12 season, and the New Orleans Hornets had failed to provide him a supporting cast worthy of a championship team. In Paul's near six years with the team, David West had been his only All-Star teammate, and the now 31-year old power forward had last made the team in 2009. West also decided to pursue the free agency market when he forwent his player option with New Orleans.

As the offseason progressed, it was becoming clearer that Chris Paul had no plans of staying in New Orleans for a long-term period. He was already in the mood to follow the footsteps of the likes of LeBron James and Chris Bosh to play on a team that had enough pieces and stars to pull together a run for the NBA championship.[vii]

As a consummate competitor, it did not seem like it was in Chris Paul's character to chase titles by teaming up with fellow superstars. He was always the kind of player that wanted to win on his terms. However, the burden of carrying a seemingly directionless New Orleans franchise for six seasons had already worn him down.

In New Orleans, Chris Paul was allowed to be the superstar he truly was. He had the ball in his hands for most of the plays as he could choose to either score the ball himself or make plays for his teammates. He was allowed to flourish and turn himself into an elite superstar in the NBA. However, the franchise did not give him a lot of tools to work with to win a title. Chris Paul, for all of his brilliance, had endured injuries and hardships in six seasons with the Hornets just to see his season end early every year. The burden and the frustrations had already become too much for him.

But Chris Paul did not want to be traded to just any team. He had preferences, and he wanted to win. His top choices boiled down to the Lakers, the Knicks, and the Magic.[vii] With the Lakers, Paul would have had a chance to team up with Kobe Bryant on an already championship-caliber squad. In New York, CP3 would have had the opportunity to play in the NBA's biggest market and under the bright lights of Madison Square Garden. Lastly, he would have also been able to team up with an equally disgruntled Dwight Howard in Orlando to create a deadly inside-outside combination.

The Hornets began to explore trading Chris Paul to another team with more potential—or rather, they would have, if the NBA had not undergone a lockout after the 2010-11 season ended. When the lockout was lifted in December, the Hornets had only a few weeks to find a suitable trading partner. It did not take long for other teams to take the bait, especially since Chris Paul was still as elite as any point guard could be.

New Orleans's first choice was the Los Angeles Lakers. On December 8, 2011, Chris Paul was traded to the Los Angeles Lakers in a three-way deal that also included the Houston Rockets. Chris Paul was slated to go to Los Angeles while Lamar Odom was supposed to go to New Orleans and Pau Gasol to the Rockets.

There were also reports that indicated the Los Angeles Lakers were trying to make a trade for Dwight Howard, who was also unhappy with his team, with Andrew Bynum as the centerpiece. The CP3 trade would have made the Lakers a powerhouse team despite losing Gasol and Odom because they were getting the best passing point guard and the most dominant center in the NBA. The trio of Kobe, Paul, and Howard could have dominated the league for a very long time and would have also contended with the Miami Heat for the mantle of the best trio in the NBA.

But just when the trade seemed to be official, many of the NBA's owners revolted. The owners had forced a lockout partly to resolve parity differences between big-market teams like the Lakers and small-market teams like the Hornets. After so much time missed with the lockout, many were outraged that the minute the lockout ended, the Lakers had grabbed another superstar. They also had leverage because in December 2010, the NBA had bought the Hornets from a broke George Shinn, which meant that the NBA's owners now collectively controlled the Hornets.

In one of the most controversial moves in basketball history, the NBA stepped in and vetoed the trade. Since the NBA owned the Hornets at that time, Commissioner David Stern had all the rights to veto the trade that could have changed the direction of the league and earned the ire of the other team owners. Had the trade not been prohibited, the Lakers could have completed their supposed quick rebuild that season because they would have centered their franchise's hopes on Chris Paul. The damage that a possible combination of Paul, Kobe, and Howard could have done would have been too devastating for the rest of the league.

The veto was unfortunately not without controversy. Reports flooded in saying that the other team owners were vehemently against the trade, just when they thought that everything was fixed during the lockout. But the commissioner was stern that his decision to veto the trade was because of basketball reasons. David Stern believed that the New Orleans Hornets were at the losing end of the deal. He wanted young and talented players in exchange for Paul to appeal the franchise to prospective buyers.[viii] Because of that, Chris Paul remained a Hornet, but everyone knew that his days in New Orleans were numbered.

Six days later, the Los Angeles Clippers stepped in and completed a trade for Paul. The Clippers sent center Chris Kaman, guard Eric Gordon, forward Al-Farouq Aminu, and the unprotected 2012 first-round pick from the Minnesota Timberwolves to the Hornets, who in turn surrendered Paul and two future second-round draft picks.

The deal that the Clippers offered to the Hornets seemed more appealing for David Stern and his quest of giving New Orleans solid rebuilding pieces for the franchise's interested bidders. Eric Gordon, who was just off from a career season, looked as though he could develop into an All-Star.[viii] On the other hand, Aminu was still young and growing at that time, and he still had enough potential in him to become a serviceable player in the league.

After the trade had been consummated, Paul announced that he would be opting in to the final year of his contract, which meant he would be with the Clippers for at least two seasons. The trade was so sudden that Clipper high flying big men Blake Griffin and DeAndre Jordan heard the news when they were out for a stroll around town. As soon as the duo heard of their new acquisition, they were ecstatic, and Griffin suddenly coined the term "lob city" in his excitement. Lob City would become the Clippers' moniker as soon as CP3 came in to change the culture of the team.

Lob City: First Season as a Clipper

For years upon years, the Los Angeles Clippers had been one of the biggest jokes in the NBA. Owner Donald Sterling had continually scrimped on the team and forced them into decades of irrelevancy. But after drafting Blake Griffin, an athletic dunking monster who had made the All-Star team as a rookie, the Clippers finally began to have positive momentum. The Clippers were already an improving franchise, even before grabbing Chris Paul from the trading block. Blake Griffin was a big revelation as a rookie, and DeAndre Jordan was quickly rising through the ranks as an athletic center. And they were also able to get two former All-Star veterans from free agency, namely Chauncey Billups and Caron Butler, and they were on the way to a slow and steady improvement. With the arrival of Chris Paul, the Clippers transformed from just another young up-and-coming squad to a team with legitimate championship aspirations. They technically went from 0 to 10 with just a flip of a switch.

With Chris Paul running the point guard spot and Blake Griffin and athletic center DeAndre Jordan as the primary big men, Los Angeles quickly lived up to their name of Lob City, a fast-paced team with great passing and lots of dunks. However, the Clippers lacked good wing players at that point, which meant that Chris Paul had to take on more of a scoring role as well. The team would later make a move for Nick Young to remedy the lack of wing scoring. Veteran power forwards were also added as a backup for the young Clipper big men.

The Clippers had a good start, especially with reliable veterans like Billups, Mo Williams, and Butler in the team mentoring the younger talents. But Chauncey, who started as a shooting guard because of Paul, would see his season end due to a torn Achilles tendon. Luckily, guys like Bledsoe, Williams, and Randy Foye were ready to take over for the injured shot-making guard.

Chris Paul would make his Clippers debut on December 25, 2011. In that game against the Golden State Warriors, Paul ran the offense to perfection to run away with the win for the Clippers. He had 20 points on only 12 shots while dishing out nine assists in the process. As good as he was in his first game with the Clippers, Paul's breakout game in LA was when he had 27 points and 11 assists in a win against the powerhouse Miami Heat squad on January 11, 2012. In the next game, he scored 33 against no less than the Los Angeles Lakers.

As good as Chris Paul was as a superstar, since the trade was so sudden and because training camp was shortened because of the lockout, Chris Paul did not have enough time to blend in with the young players and to adjust to the system that head coach Vinny Del Negro wanted with the Clippers. Moreover, the 66-game season was so compressed that it hindered teams from getting enough rest between games. Because of that and since Billups' injury, the Clippers went on to lose a lot of games, which made people ponder the future of Del Negro as the head coach of the newest star-laden team in the NBA.

No matter the system or coach, Chris Paul had seemingly regained his status as the best pure point guard in the NBA because of the move to Los Angeles. While teammates like Blake Griffin, Caron Butler, Mo Williams, and DeAndre Jordan were making life easier for him, it was still the brilliance of CP3's ability to run teams that got him back to elite status and made the Los Angeles Clippers the newest contenders in the Western Conference.

In his first season as a Clipper, Chris Paul averaged 19.8 points and 9.1 assists per game throughout the 2011-12 season. He was nominated for his fifth All-Star Game as well as the All-Defensive Team and was the first Clipper ever to be placed on the All-NBA First Team. He and Griffin were the first duo of All-Stars in Clippers history. Los Angeles Clippers leaped up the standings, going from winning 32 games in an 82-game season in 2010-11 to winning 40 games in a 66 game season. It is amazing how one player can entirely change the culture of one team. Chris Paul is and was always that kind of a player.

The Clippers faced the Memphis Grizzlies in the first round of the NBA playoffs. The Grizzlies were one of the most, if not the most, physical teams in the NBA, and they always made it a point to pound the ball inside on offense and to pressure the ball handler on defense. Luckily, the Clips had Paul manning the ball-handling duties. An All-Star point guard like CP3 is capable enough to handle the pressure that Memphis puts on point guards.

Despite not having home-court advantage entering the series, the Clippers stole the advantage by winning Game 1. Their midseason acquisition Nick Young immediately paid dividends off the bench by scoring 19. The Clipper bench was the difference-maker in the game, especially when LA was down by as much as 21 entering the final quarter. Young ignited the rally when the Grizzlies thought they were able to take care handily of the Clipper starters. Though playing a little subpar, Paul was able to score 14 points and distribute the ball for 11 baskets.

Los Angeles was thinking of stealing both home games away from the Grizzlies, but Memphis would have none of it. After winning the first quarter, the Los Angeles Clippers went on to lose the next three quarters as well as the whole game. Paul and Griffin exploded with 29 and 22 respectively, but all the other Clipper starters were useless on the floor. Meanwhile, it was the Memphis bench that annihilated the Clips' reserves.

In LA for Game 3, the Clippers were down again entering the fourth quarter. With a 9-0 run in the final three minutes, the Clips got a 6-point lead that was trimmed down to 1 point after two desperation shots by Rudy Gay and after LA missed free throw after free throw. But when the game was in its dying seconds and with the ball in possession of Memphis, Gay tried another outside shot, but it missed. The Clippers were barely able to win the game, 87 to 86. Paul had 24 points and 11 assists while Gay had 24 for Memphis.

In another tight game in Los Angeles, the Grizzlies played the Clippers wire-to-wire until the match was forced into overtime. It was also a classic duel of young point guards: Chris Paul versus Mike Conley. Both point guards almost had triple-doubles. Paul recorded 27, 9, and seven while Conley had 25, 7, and 8. In the end, the better point guard triumphed, and the Clippers won the game 101 to 97 in overtime.

With the Clips up 3-1 in the series, they needed only one win to get to the second round and suddenly make the Clippers legitimate winners in the NBA. But people began to think that the Clips suddenly went back to their losing culture when they lost the next two games and had to try to win the series in a dangerous Game 7. Whether the LA Clippers went back to their losing ways or whether the Grizzlies were just grittier in those two games are questions that did not need to be answered then because winning Game 7 was much more important for LA.

Defense was always the Grizzlies' best facet. It was their ticket to winning games, and nobody played that end of the court better. But for one important game, the Clippers were the better defensive team. LA played the gritty style of defense that made Memphis a dangerous team to limit the Grizzlies throughout four quarters of physical basketball. Memphis was also able to defend the Clippers at the highest level possible; the problem was that the Grizzlies forgot about the Clipper bench.

With both starting lineups struggling, the Los Angeles bench suddenly stormed out in the fourth quarter to build a 10-point cushion. The bench was playing so well that Del Negro opted to play them the majority of the final quarter. Meanwhile, Memphis' bench was not as productive. In the end, the Clippers were able to hold on to the 10-point win thanks to their deep bench. As the lone bright spot in the starting lineup, Paul had 19 points and nine rebounds.

But in the second round, Chris Paul once again faced the San Antonio Spurs, who had trounced the Utah Jazz in the first round and had won their last 14 straight games. The Spurs were playing their best basketball in recent years despite the aging core of Duncan, Parker, and Ginobili leading the team. While a lot of people thought that the Clippers would give a better fight than the Jazz could muster up, the Spurs were just at the point that they could not care any less who was standing in their way.

The Clippers became just a speed bump for the surging Spurs and were swept out of the 2012 NBA playoffs. It was never even close. The Spurs won the first two games in San Antonio by a total of 33 points. In the two games, CP3 only averaged 8 points. That was his worst two-game playoff stretch. Game 3 in LA was no different. The Spurs won it by 10 points, and Chris only scored 12. In that three-game stretch, it seemed as if Tony Parker was easily the better point guard. Game 4 was the best that CP3 and the Clippers would play against the Spurs. However, their best was not enough. They would lose the game 103 to 99, and it was the closest game of the series. With the win, the Spurs advanced to the Western Conference Finals, and the Clippers were off to go fishing in the summer. In his first playoff appearance with the LA Clippers, Chris Paul averaged 17.6 points, 5.1 rebounds, and 7.9 assists.

Rising with the Clippers

In the offseason following the loss to the Spurs, Chris Paul activated his player option, which would make him a free agent in 2013, but would keep him as a Clipper for one more season. While everyone knew that he would almost certainly sign a new deal with the Clippers in 2013, a disappointing playoff performance might have made him think otherwise. The Clippers brought in Grant Hill and Jamaal Crawford to bolster their wing rotation. They also acquired hard-nosed defender Matt Barnes to play the small forward position behind Caron Butler. Former Lakers Lamar Odom and Ronny Turiaf were also able to make their return to Los Angeles but as Clippers. Odom, a former champion and former Sixth Man of the Year, would become a good backup for Griffin and Jordan.

With the Clippers' new acquisitions and with their chemistry intact due to a longer training camp, Los Angeles' "second" team was quickly become the better team in the city as the Lakers struggled to mesh their superstars Dwight Howard, Kobe Bryant, Pau Gasol, and Steve Nash together. Of course, everything started and ended with Chris Paul and his brilliance in leading a team and heading an offense.

Chris Paul started the season with three consecutive good performances, finishing all three games with double-double performances on points and assists. He was then instrumental in leading the Clippers to an 8-2 start in their first ten games. That was their best start as a franchise in league history. The Los

Angeles Clippers were 14-6 through their first 20 games, especially because of CP3's abilities in running a team.

The Clippers were even so good that they were able to win 17 straight games early in the season. That 17-win stretch was the best streak in Clippers history. Their previous win streak record was at 8. They doubled that streak in the 2012-13 season. And in the middle of that 17-game winning streak was Paul brandishing his elite level skills and leadership. He had nine double-doubles in that stretch of wins.

With the presence of Crawford as well as the development of backup point guard Eric Bledsoe, Paul's minutes dropped to the lowest of his career at 33 minutes per game. But everything was still well for the Clippers because of the newfound confidence the team suddenly saw. Even with Paul out because of a bruised kneecap he had suffered in a game against the Orlando Magic, the Los Angeles Clippers were still winning. However, it was obvious that Paul was the presence that kept the Clippers together. The team struggled with a 6-6 record in the 12 games that CP3 missed between January and February.

Chris Paul's return to the lineup ignited the Los Angeles Clippers to a strong rally as the season was nearing its end. In an ultra-competitive Western Conference setting, the Clippers were surprisingly one of the contenders for the top spots. In the middle of it was CP3 who kept on getting his teammates involved with his ability break down offenses and to get open looks for others.

Chris Paul averaged 16.9 points, and 9.7 assists per game and was once again nominated to start in the 2013 All-Star Game, where he won his first NBA All-Star MVP award by leading the Western Conference team to a 143-138 victory while scoring 20 points, dishing off 15 assists, and picking up four steals. With Paul's stellar play and the success his team was seeing, Chris Paul was again on pace to regaining the status of best point guard in the world, particularly since Derrick Rose was struggling with injury. But Paul was barely holding on to that title because Westbrook and Stephen Curry were quickly rising through the ranks.

However, CP3 was still the league's best pure point guard, especially because of his unparalleled ability at running an offense though he was not as explosive as Westbrook, Rose, or John Wall. He had a total of 31 double-doubles on points and assists the entire season while shooting 48.1% from the floor. Though his scoring was down to the second lowest in his career, it was not due to a lack of effort on his part on the offensive end, but rather because he focused on getting his teammates involved. He only attempted about 12 shots a game that year.

At season's end, Paul was once again rewarded with a spot on the All-NBA First team and the NBA All-Defensive First team. For the first time in history, the Clippers swept their regular-season matchup with the Lakers. There was indeed a changing of the guard in LA. The Clippers had the best season in franchise history with 56 regular season victories as well as their first-ever Pacific Division title. It was their first 50-win season, and they were good enough to have the fourth seed in the competitive Western Conference. They were going to match up once again with the Memphis Grizzlies. However, this time, they were the ones that had home-court advantage.

Much like last season's first-round battle between the Clippers and the Grizzlies, home-court advantage was useless. While the Clippers won Game 1 in a 21-point blowout fashion because of CP3's 23 points and Game 2 by 2 points with Paul again playing a stellar role, the Grizzlies went on to take revenge in the two games in Memphis. In the two wins in Tennessee, the Grizzlies' Marc Gasol and Zach Randolph severely outmatched the Clipper frontline of Griffin and Jordan. Blake and DeAndre could do nothing to stop the two behemoths from lording over them in the paint as Memphis won their two straight home games by double digits.

Chris Paul exploded in Game 5 out of the sense of urgency because the series was basically down to a best of three. Paul scored 35 points to outplay his counterpart Mike Conley in their second straight playoff series matchup. But Memphis went back to their bread and butter. The tandem of Gasol and Randolph dominated the paint once again, and the duo had 46 points. Meanwhile, Griffin and Jordan combined for 10 points, and it was a one-man show for the Clippers as the Grizzlies went on to win their third straight game to lead the series 3-2.

With Griffin playing on a sprained ankle, the Clippers seemed to be the underdogs in Game 6, a do-or-die situation for them. With the Clippers playing desperately, the Grizzlies relied on Randolph once again. LA was still struggling to find points from their starters, and only CP3 was keeping them alive, aside from Matt Barnes scoring big off the bench. But Conley, together with bench players Quincy Pondexter and Bayless, matched Paul and Barnes' output. It was evident that Lionel Hollins was outcoaching Del Negro throughout the series, and the Clippers looked very confused on the floor. In the end, the Clips bowed down the Grizzlies 105 to 118. After winning two straight games, LA went on to lose four straight and fingers were pointing to head coach Vinny del Negro for the first-round exit.

Enter Doc Rivers

Paul was a free agent in the 2013 offseason, and he explored his options. When the Houston Rockets signed Dwight Howard, Paul briefly considered joining Howard as well as All-Star guard James Harden. Determined to keep Paul happy, the Clippers dramatically overhauled their roster.

As expected due to their four straight losses to the Grizzlies, coach Vinny Del Negro was fired, and after a series of lengthy negotiations with the Boston Celtics, who wanted to start their franchise fresh, they obtained a highly respected coach in Doc Rivers. The trade for Doc Rivers was an unprecedented move not only in franchise history, but also in the annals of the NBA. Swapping a coach to another team was almost unheard of. But the Clippers, intent on making their team better, made the move for Rivers by trading away a first round pick.

Doc Rivers won a championship in 2008 with the Celtics and was famous for his ability to handle the egos of All-Star players Kevin Garnett, Paul Pierce, Ray Allen, and Rajon Rondo. Moreover, Doc also played a big part in helping Rondo develop into arguably the best assisting point guard in the NBA. With

Rivers mentoring Chris Paul, one could only speculate how much better Paul would become.

The Clips also traded Eric Bledsoe for wingman Jared Dudley and obtained sharpshooter J.J. Redick to help alleviate pressure in the paint because of his ability to stretch the floor. The aging Caron Butler was also part of that deal. Happy with how Matt Barnes brought a lot of defensive toughness, the Clippers renewed him for another two seasons.

Having traded their backup point guard, they also signed Darren Collison, whose best season had been playing behind Chris Paul in New Orleans when he was but a rookie. Satisfied with the changes, Paul re-signed with the Clippers on a five-year, $107 million deal. The Clippers had secured their superstar and franchise cornerstone. They were also in possession of arguably the most dominant power forward in the league in Blake Griffin and an ultra-athletic center in DeAndre Jordan. But could they finally win a title?

As the 2013-14 season began, the Clippers were viewed as one of the best, if not the most complete, team in the Western Conference, and perhaps the NBA. They had excellent shooters in Redick and Dudley, a good big man pair in Griffin and Jordan, one of the best coaches in the league in Doc Rivers, and arguably the best pure point guard in the game with Chris Paul. One could argue that the only weakness in the team was their small forward rotation.

Nevertheless, the Los Angeles Clippers were starting to get better not only because of Doc Rivers, but because of the emergence of the other key players as well. Blake Griffin was norming his usual dominant scoring numbers again while DeAndre Jordan was rising as one of the most promising centers in the NBA. More importantly, Chris Paul, with the full trust of Rivers, was back to running the show on his terms once again. His performances were getting better and better under the new coach than they ever were under Del Negro.

The new look Clippers started the season strong having won the majority of their first few games. Running the machine was Chris Paul, who would have 13 consecutive double-double performances on points and assists at the start of the new season. CP3 was not only scoring at a good pace, but was also running the offense to perfection as he made everyone on the roster look good because of his ability to make the right plays.

As the season progressed, Paul was only getting better while adjusting to the new system that Doc Rivers wanted to implement to the Clippers. In one of the most efficient games one could ever see, Chris Paul poured in 38 points and 12 assists in only about 33 minutes of action in a win over the Washington Wizards on December 14, 2013. Matched up against the younger, bigger, and more athletic point guard John Wall, Chris Paul still outplayed his counterpart as he proved that he was still the best at his position.

With Chris Paul and the Los Angeles Clippers playing at an all-time franchise high, it seemed like they were on their way to one of the best seasons in team history. What could derail them? Unfortunately, the answer turned out to be injuries. Redick only played 35 games that season, and on January 3, 2014, Paul suffered a separated shoulder against the Dallas Mavericks. He was forced to sit out for over a month.

Moreover, their hole at the small forward position turned out to be a huge problem. Though Barnes was a terrific defender and a reliable outside shooter, he could not provide a lot of wing scoring. Hence, the Clippers signed a bunch of veteran small forwards to try to fill that hole. They first acquired Stephen Jackson, but the veteran scorer could not stay healthy and would play only nine games before being waived.

Next, Hedo Türkoğlu was signed from the free agency market. Though Hedo was no longer the versatile forward he was in

Orlando, he still provided good playmaking and defense off the bench. Lastly, former All-Star wingman Danny Granger was signed in late February. The team also acquired capable big man Glen Davis before signing Granger.

However, Paul's injury turned out to be a blessing in disguise. With Paul out, Blake Griffin was forced to carry the Clippers on his back. Griffin had been criticized as just another flashy dunker and a one-trick pony. But while Paul rested and recovered, Griffin stepped up and proved himself to be one of the most complete power forwards in the NBA.

The athletic big man developed into a capable perimeter shooter, and his post game was slowly improving. Aside from his offensive arsenal, Griffin developed into one of the best playmaking big men in the NBA, averaging nearly four assists for the season. Aside from Griffin's rise, DeAndre Jordan would also drastically improve after getting a vote of confidence from coach Doc Rivers.

Under Del Negro, Jordan was not playing at full capacity concerning minutes because of his limited offensive repertoire. But Rivers accepted DJ's weakness on the offensive end because he loved his athleticism and defense. He became one of the best rebounders and shot blockers in the league, improving to 13.6 rebounds and 2.5 blocks for the season. He was also the most efficient field goal shooter in the NBA with 67.6% from the floor as he was the recipient of many lob passes from Paul and Griffin.

The Clippers managed to go 12-6 while Paul was out. When he returned, the revitalized duo of CP3 and Griffin tore up the NBA on offense while DJ focused on rebounding and paint protection. The Clippers won 13 out of 15 games in March, and secured the Pacific Division for the second straight year.

On his part, Chris Paul did not look like he missed a beat because of the injury. He immediately went back to his usual work of controlling the tempo for the Clippers and of making life easier for his teammates on the offensive end. His numbers since his return were a testament to how well he was playing despite the month-long absence from any basketball activities. Despite the injuries to Paul, Redick, and other players, the Clippers managed to win 57 games—a one-game improvement from the last year and another franchise high for wins.

Paul averaged 19.1 points, 10.7 assists, and 2.5 steals for the 2013-14 season. He was easily another All-Star along with Blake. He also bagged his fourth All-NBA First Team selection as well as his third straight All-Defensive First Team nomination. Paul also led the league in steals for the fourth consecutive season. And after four years of not leading the league in assists, Chris Paul was once again the best passer in the league that season for the third time in his career. With his steady play at his position and with the Clippers winning games after games, Chris Paul was still the best point guard in the NBA after temporarily ceding that accolade to Derrick Rose for at least one year.

The Clippers faced off against the Golden State Warriors in the first round of the 2014 NBA playoffs. Like the Clippers, the Warriors also used to be a cellar dweller team, but were quickly rising through the ranks because of their young shooting duo, Stephen Curry and Klay Thompson, also known as the "Splash Brothers." Curry was an up-and-coming point guard known for his unbelievable shooting and his sick ball handling ability. He was one of the players contending to steal away Paul's title as the best point guard in the world. However, for all his unearthly shooting abilities and flashy handles, Steph Curry was not Chris Paul.

As Game 1 unfolded, CP3 outplayed his younger, inexperienced counterpart. Paul was shooting better than Steph Curry and was also instrumental in making everyone else look better. But the Warriors had several other weapons to rely on and they were able to fend off a late rally by the Clippers to win the game, 109 to 105. Paul had 28 points and eight assists.

The Clippers took revenge in a big way in the following match. They set two franchise playoff records. First, they scored an incredible 138 points; second, their winning margin of 40 points was also a record. Though Steph outplayed Paul the entirety of Game 2, all the other Clippers, especially Griffin, rampaged all over the Warriors. CP3 finished that historic game with 12 points, ten assists, and five steals while playing only 27 minutes.

In Game 3, the star point guards once again dueled to a stalemate. They were technically canceling out each other in a very close game. But it was once again Griffin, after carrying the Clips the majority of the regular season, who lorded over the Warriors with 32 points to win the close game 98 to 96. Paul had 15 and ten while Curry had 16 and 15. But the Warriors would not allow the Clippers to win two games in the Bay Area as Curry exploded for 33 points in Game 4 against Paul's 16 in a blowout victory for the Warriors. This loss came after team owner Donald Sterling was in the headlines.

Sterling, who had a history of being racist, was receiving a lot of backlash from the public after reports broke out of his racial discrimination against African-Americans. The Clippers were composed primarily of African-American players, but it seemed like they did not even have the support of their team owner, who had different opinions and views about races other than his own. The team was so affected by the news that it contributed to their Game 4 loss.

With the series down to a best of three, the Clippers drew first blood with a well-balanced attack that featured a breakout playoff performance from DeAndre Jordan, who had 25 points and 18 rebounds. Paul had 20 points and seven assists in the 10-point victory. Despite being only one win away from advancing to the second round, the Clippers would suffer a heartbreaking loss due to a late game 3-pointer by Andre Iguodala, who helped the Warriors win by 1 point. The win came after the NBA announcing that Donald Sterling was banned for a lifetime from the NBA. Sterling was also forced by the NBA commissioner to sell his ownership of the Clippers, and thus ended the Sterling era.

As the game was down to a do-or-die Game 7, the Warriors came out firing, and they led by eight at the end of the first half. The Clippers somehow got it going in the third quarter to get the lead heading into the fourth. With both teams scoring in bunches in the fourth quarter, the Clippers maintained to be the hotter team, especially with four players scoring more than 20 points. In the end, Los Angeles held on to a five-point win on the strength of a balanced attack. Paul scored 22 and assisted on 14 baskets though Curry, who had 33 and 9, outplayed him. Nevertheless, the important part was that he and the Clippers advanced to the next round.

If the Clippers thought that the Warriors duo was difficult to guard against, they were headed to face a tougher pair of superstars. Their second-round opponents were the Oklahoma City Thunder led by the NBA scoring leader and brand new MVP Kevin Durant and the most ferocious point guard Russell Westbrook. KD had the best season in his career and was the rightful MVP winner. Meanwhile, Westbrook was limited by injuries, but was still the league's most dynamic point guard and was arguably the fastest and most athletic player pound-for-pound in the NBA. Paul was once again up against a point guard ready to take away the top point guard spot.

While the difficulties in guarding Kevin Durant was left to the wingmen of the Clippers, the immediate problem facing CP3 in that series matchup was stopping Russell Westbrook. Though Paul was still the best pure playmaker in the league, Westbrook was one of the other point guards that could give CP3 a run for his money as far as the other aspects of the game were concerned. He was bigger, stronger, faster, and light-years more athletic than any other player at his position. However, Chris Paul was just as competitive as Westbrook on top of being the more controlled and more experienced player between the two.

In Game 1 versus the Thunder, Paul proved that he was up to the challenge of making life equally difficult for his matchup by making a career playoff-best eight three-pointers as the Clippers drew first blood. He was so hot that he scored 32 points and still managed to get ten assists as the Clips won the opening game by 17 to steal home-court advantage. CP3 only played 27 minutes in that match.

Unfortunately for Chris Paul, he could not replicate the same magic he had in Game 1. In Game 2, he only finished with 17 points and ten assists while also struggling to contain Russell Westbrook. With Paul probably not at his best after the 32-point explosion, it was Westbrook's turn to play big. Russ had 31 points and a triple-double to help the Thunder tie the series.

In the first game in Los Angeles, the Clippers had a monumental fourth-quarter breakdown that ceded home-court advantage once again to the Thunder. The reigning NBA MVP was just incredible, scoring 36 points. Meanwhile, Paul and Westbrook canceled each other out as they both scored more than 20 and assisted on more than ten baskets. The Clippers battled back to tie the series at two games apiece on the strength of their fourth-quarter comeback, fueled by their bench. They would survive KD's 40-point output in Game 4 with Chris Paul putting up 23 points and ten assists in that game.

In the crucial Game 5, Paul committed a series of blunders in the match's final seconds that would lead to their playoff demise once again. Paul, who had 17 points and 14 assists, had five turnovers, including two crucial ones in the final 4 minutes as the Thunder charged once again to a fourth-quarter rally.

Protecting a slim 104-102 lead with 17 seconds left, Chris Paul lost the ball after thinking that Russell Westbrook would foul him after receiving the inbounds pass. That turnover resulted in a steal by Reggie Jackson and an out-of-bounds play with OKC retaining ball possession. During the Thunder's final possession in the ensuing play, Paul uncharacteristically fouled Russell Westbrook while Westbrook was taking a 3-point shot, and the Thunder PG made all three foul shots to give OKC a 1- point lead.

Not only did Paul commit blunders, but he was also severely outclassed by Westbrook, who scored 38. Facing elimination in Game 6, the Clippers raced to a 14-point lead in the first quarter. Unfortunately, the Thunder was just too good to allow the

Clippers to maintain that lead. After cutting the lead in the second quarter and taking over the game in the third, OKC fended off the Clippers in the final quarter to finally end Los Angeles' dreams of getting past the second round. Though Paul had 25 points and 11 assists, Kevin Durant was unstoppable with 39.

With the loss to the Thunder in that series, Chris Paul once again saw his playoff run ending in the second round. Nevertheless, he had a terrific series against the OKC Thunder despite the difficulties he faced in matching with Westbrook. He averaged 22.5 points, 11.8 assists, and 2.5 steals the entire series while never failing to record a double-double in every outing of that six-game matchup. Unfortunately, there was still something missing in the Clippers even though their leader and best player was playing to his full capacity.

Though Chris Paul lost that series, it was evident to everyone's mind that CP3 was at the top of his game and the top of his class. Pound for pound, no other point guard came close to his skills and abilities in leading a team. Though he was recognized by many as the best point guard in the NBA at that time, Chris Paul was still playing with a chip on his shoulder during the playoffs.

At barely 6-feet tall, Chris Paul chased the 6'3" Stephen Curry all throughout the floor and through difficult screens just to get a hand up on the prolific shooter during the grueling and tough series against the Golden State Warriors. And on mismatch situations, he was often matched up with the 6'7" Klay Thompson, but he never gave an inch to the bigger and taller guard.

That he tried to outplay the larger and faster Russell Westbrook at every facet of the game during the second round against the Oklahoma City Thunder was proof to how competitive and mature Chris Paul was as a leader and elite player. Physically, one would understand that CP3 was on the losing end of every matchup he has seen in the NBA. The one skill that Paul owned was that he knew how to see weaknesses and use them to his advantage. That was made him special.

On the floor, Paul made it a point to exploit weaknesses and open spots on the court. Off the floor, he made sure that his teammates were on the same page and mindset as he was. During the playoffs, there was never any dead air on the bench when Chris Paul was sitting on it. He habitually advised teammates as if he was an extension of the head coach himself. He always made sure that his team had the tactical advantage even when he was not playing.

And though the Los Angeles Clippers eventually lost the war against the OKC Thunder, the bright side was that Chris Paul had fully grown into his role as a leader. Statistically, he was at his peak. But it was his maturity that got the respect he rightfully deserved during that postseason run. And while he was yet again eluded by that championship ring he sorely needed to solidify his name as one of the best point guards the league has ever seen, CP3's growth and maturity that season was going to be the Clippers' best weapon in the franchise's quest for a title in the future.

Steve Ballmer Era, Challenged at the Top of the Point Guard Crop

The Clippers retained their core players for the 2014-15 NBA season and added a few other capable role players to the bench. Moreover, former Microsoft CEO Steve Ballmer bought the Clippers and brought new ownership enthusiasm that rivaled Dallas Mavericks' owner Mark Cuban.

With billionaire owner Steve Ballmer enthusiastically cheering the team on from the sidelines, the Los Angeles Clippers opened the 2014-15 season full of confidence against the Oklahoma City Thunder, who eliminated them in the previous season. The Thunder were without Kevin Durant, who was sidelined with a Jones fracture, and then they had to play without point guard Russell Westbrook from the second quarter onwards because of a broken hand fracture.

But OKC fought hard behind Perry Jones and Serge Ibaka, taking the Clippers to the limit before Blake Griffin's two free throws iced the 93-90 win. Griffin topped the Clippers in scoring with 23 points, but it was Chris Paul's dominant effort on both ends of the floor that spelled the difference. Paul did not just score 22 points and issue 7 assists, he also had four rebounds, three steals, and one block to set the tone for what would be another remarkable all-around statistical season for the league's best point guard.

In their fourth game of the season, Chris Paul recorded the first triple-double of the season and his first ever as a member of the Clippers. Paul had 13 points, 12 assists, and ten rebounds in a 107-101 home win against the Utah Jazz. But while Paul was starting to show his overall brilliance early on in the season, the team struggled, going just 4-4 after their opening night victory over the Thunder.

While things were not going as planned, Ballmer's "Hardcore" Clippers were not unfazed. After all, they were just one game off from the previous season's 6-3 start and had also opened the

2013 season at 8-6. Chris Paul then took charge of the Clippers' offense and averaged 10.42 assists in the next 12 games as the Clippers went 11-1, including a 9-game winning streak. The Clippers never went below nine games over the .500 mark the rest of the season.

Chris Paul, once again, was putting up a fantastic season on top of playing at his healthiest state in his 10-year career. While we were always accustomed to seeing Paul banged up at some point in the season, CP3 never seemed bothered by the many injuries he faced over his decade-long career. He was at full health while putting up the numbers he usually averaged every season. Along with his maturity as a leader, Paul had finally learned how to take care of his body as he unloaded himself of all the burdens of carrying the Clippers thanks to the overall effort of his teammates.

With Chris Paul playing at his best and healthiest, the Los Angeles Clippers were once again one of the contenders for the top spots in the Western Conference playoff picture. While CP3 made it a point not to let teams forget how good of a scorer he always was, his primary goal throughout the season was to make sure his teammates were also playing confidently and on the top of their respective games. Key players such as DeAndre Jordan, JJ Redick, Matt Barnes, and Jamal Crawford were playing beyond their standard capabilities thanks to the efforts of their star point guard.

But the Clippers' quest for success encountered a roadblock in February when Blake Griffin suffered a staph infection in his right elbow. At the time of the injury, Griffin was leading the Clippers in scoring at 22.5 points per game while averaging 7.5 rebounds and a career-high 5.1 assists per game. The Clippers were 13.7 points better per 100 possessions with Griffin on the floor and also shot the ball 5.2% better with him around. In Griffin's absence, center DeAndre Jordan stepped up his game big time, averaging 14.6 points and 18.4 rebounds per game. But it was Chris Paul who continued to play excellently on both ends of the floor for the Clippers. Paul averaged 22.0 points and 13.4 assists in Griffin's absence and was the key to keeping the Clippers afloat with a 9-6 record during that time.

On February 15, 2015, Chris Paul played in his eighth consecutive All-Star game, where he tallied a game-high 15 assists with 12 points and two steals in 26 minutes of action. His Western Conference team won the Game 163-158, but it was Russell Westbrook who took home MVP honors by his 41 points scored. On March 11, 2015, Paul outplayed Westbrook in their third meeting of the season. CP3 scored 33 points on 11 of 19 shooting and held Russell Westbrook to 2 for eight from the field and seven turnovers when he was guarding the OKC stalwart. Before that game, Westbrook was on his unprecedented triple-double tear at that time and had scored 40 points six times since February 6. But Paul clearly outplayed him, not just by producing better numbers, but also by stopping Westbrook on the defensive end. Clearly, Chris Paul had emerged as an elite defender, and this would be rewarded with a spot on the NBA's All-Defensive First team.

On April 1, Paul had a season high of 41 points and delivered 17 assists plus four steals and five rebounds as the Clippers rallied to beat the Portland Trail Blazers 126-22 in a victory that sparked the Clippers to win their last seven regular season games, and 14 of their last 15 to finish at 56-26. The strong finish enabled the Pacific Division Champion Clippers to secure the third seed and home-court advantage in the first round of the 2015 NBA playoffs. However, the third spot meant that the Clippers had to face the San Antonio Spurs in Round 1 of the playoffs since the Spurs fell from the second seed to sixth after dropping their final regular season assignment against the New Orleans Pelicans. The Clippers-Spurs series would be one for the ages.

Chris Paul opened the series with 32 points, seven rebounds, six assists, and 3 of 5 shooting from 3-point distance as the Clippers drew first blood, 107-92. With that performance, it seemed like CP3 was hungrier for a title than all of the other San Antonio Spurs players combined. There was nothing the Spurs could do to stop him from tearing up the defenses in that game.

Unfortunately for Paul, things would get tougher from then on. He would have a respectable output of 21 points, eight rebounds, and seven assists while shooting above 50% in Game 2. However, the rest of the Clippers struggled against the top defense of the world champions. While the starters were playing well, the bench was awful in that loss. Game 3 was even more dreadful not only for Paul but the whole Clippers as well. San Antonio put the clamps on the Clippers to win the game by 27. CP3 had an awful performance of 7 points and four assists in that devastating loss.

Ever the competitive athlete that never backed down from any challenge, Chris Paul would force his way out of the slump. After the defending champions had stormed back with two consecutive wins, Paul had 34 points and seven assists to help the Clippers even the series up at two games apiece with a 114-105 win in Game 4. The Spurs threatened the Clippers anew by winning the crucial Game 5. It was a close game where CP3 poured in 19 points and ten assists for his first double-double performance of the playoffs. His efforts, however, were not enough to get the series lead back from the Spurs. But Paul had 19 points and 15 assists to help them send the series to a deciding Game 7. However, despite having the momentum, history was not on the side of Chris Paul's Clippers. The team had not won a 7-game series when trailing 3-2. It was time to erase that history.

On a day when boxing held the biggest fight in the sports history, Mayweather-Pacquiao, the real mega-fight happened at the Staples Center when the Clippers played the Spurs in the deciding game of their first-round playoff series. With both teams hitting one big shot after another, the most competitive pairing of the 2015 playoffs came down to five-time champion Tim Duncan and the Clippers' leader Chris Paul.

Hobbling from a hamstring injury that had been bothering him, Chris Paul refused to lose the game and the series. Struggling even to run at his maximum, Paul broke down the perimeter defense to get into the lane. Once he got near enough, he jumped from his healthy but off leg and banked a running shot over Duncan with one second left to give the Clippers a pulsating 111-109 victory over the defending champions. One play earlier, the ageless Duncan hit two free throws with 8.8 seconds left to tie the game at 109-109. This happened after both teams exchanged leads in the final minutes of the match.

Paul scored 18 of his 27 points in the second half, including four key 3-pointers and that winning basket as he willed himself back from a first-half injury. The win sent the Clippers to a second-round date with the second-seeded Houston Rockets.

The hamstring injury sidelined Paul for the first two games of the second round, but the Clippers still managed a split and took the home-court advantage away from James Harden's Rockets. Paul returned in Game 3, and despite averaging just 14 points and 9.5 assists in the next two games, his mere presence and leadership inspired the Clippers to win both games by an average of 29 points.

But just when the Clippers were on the cusp of greatness with a 3-1 lead, the Rockets and MVP candidate James Harden found their stroke and won the next three games to eliminate the Clippers in seven games and reach the Western Conference Finals for the first time since 1997. It was only the 9th time in NBA history where a team came from 3-1 down to win a 7-game series and it was more painful that it happened to the Clippers, who had been playing their best basketball of the season in the first four games of the series only to collapse in the last three games. None was more disappointing than blowing a 19-point third quarter lead in Game 6 at home. In the end, the loss marked ten consecutive seasons and seven straight playoffs appearances without a trip to the Western Conference Finals.

The series breakdown could not be attributed to Chris Paul in any way. Even though he hobbled throughout the series because of his hamstring injury, the elite point guard tried his best to contribute in the best way he could. He averaged terrific numbers of 26.3 points and 10.3 assists in the final three games of the series. However, all three of those games were the losses that sent the Clippers packing home. Nevertheless, nobody could fault Paul for the performance he put up against the Thunder as he tried to send his team past the second round for the very first time.

Even in their most painful playoff exit ever, there were a lot of positives for the Clippers. One was the emergence of DeAndre Jordan as a force and future All-Star, and the other was Chris Paul establishing his health. Paul played in all 82 regular-season games for the first time in his 10-year NBA career and would have played all their games except for the first two games of the Rockets' series. He aggravated a hamstring injury by playing in the Game 7 against the Spurs in the previous round.

In a year where Stephen Curry dominated with his offensive brilliance, Chris Paul set a career high with 139 3-pointers made during the regular season and his 39.8% 3-pointer clip was his second best to date. Before the 2014-15 season, Paul had not made 100 total 3-pointers in one basketball year. During the playoffs, Paul became just the 31st player in NBA history to shoot 50% from the field, 40% from the three-point line, and 90% from the foul line during an entire postseason.

Chris Paul re-asserted himself as one of the best point guards in the NBA by leading the league in assists and steals for the fourth and sixth times in his career, respectively. Paul averaged 19.1 points and 10.2 assists per game, and it was the fifth consecutive season he had a double-double average. His 838 assists during the regular season were the most ever by a Clipper, and it allowed Paul to join Magic Johnson, Oscar Robertson, and Isiah Thomas in a very exclusive group of players that had accumulated 13,000 career points and 6,500 career assists in 700 games or fewer. For the third consecutive season, Paul also led the league with a 4.1 assists-to-turnover ratio, proving that he is the most efficient player in the league. Aside from his inclusion on the NBA's All-Defensive team, Paul was also named to the All-NBA 2nd Team for only the second time in his career. However, Chris Paul's title as the best point guard was quickly being taken away by 2015 MVP Steph Curry.

Stephen Curry was not the only one asserting himself over Chris Paul regarding supremacy at the point guard position. Russell Westbrook, who led the league in scoring and triple-doubles that season, was becoming one of the deadliest one-man forces in the league. His overall skills were seen to have exceeded that of Chris Paul's that season. Kyrie Irving, who was off from his first trip to the NBA Finals, could have also given Paul a run for his money as far as breaking down defenses was concerned. Wrapping up the rising point guard crop in the era where the position was arguably at its best were youngsters Damian Lillard, John Wall, Eric Bledsoe, and Isiah Thomas, among others.

Despite playing at his peak in the era where the point guard position was dominating the NBA, Chris Paul's mantle as an elite playmaker was still up for grabs as the competitive leader of the Los Angeles Clippers was still at his finest concerning health and maturity. At the age of 30 years old, he was not getting any younger and yet he could outplay any other point guard in the league at any given day. Pound-for-pound, Chris Paul was still the cream of the crop as far as the point guard position was concerned.

Singlehandedly Leading the Charge, Early Exits

Despite all the impressive individual accolades in his career, Paul insists that everything has been driven by his desire to win the ultimate prize: an NBA title ring. With another heartbreaker of a season, Paul said that all he needed to do was to be stronger and get better. To help him, the team upgraded during the 2015 offseason and added the likes of Paul Pierce, Josh Smith, Lance Stephenson, Wesley Johnson, Pablo Prigioni, and Chuck Hayes. However, they would lose their toughest small forward, Matt Barnes. But the team's future nearly took a twist with DeAndre Jordan's free agency.

After some serious courting from team owner Mark Cuban and persuasion from forward Chandler Parsons, DeAndre Jordan initially agreed in principle to a four-year maximum contract deal with the Dallas Mavericks. But in an unprecedented turn of events, Jordan reneged on the Dallas deal to sign an $88M deal with the Clippers. Jordan's change of heart came after Los Angeles Clippers team owner Steve Ballmer, President and Coach Doc Rivers, Blake Griffin, Paul Pierce, and Chris Paul held DeAndre Jordan "hostage" inside his home in Houston. But while Paul said publicly that he was "unbelievably" happy that his "little brother" Jordan was back, the reason why the DJ initially wanted to leave was rumored to be Chris Paul himself.

Paul's dominating personality and ultra-competitiveness reportedly drove Jordan away. It is no secret that CP3 plays way bigger than his size, and he does that with his heart. The problem is that the rift between the two started to grow during the season, because as the story went, Paul was too much of a perfectionist for DJ to handle. In short, instead of getting a "high five" from Chris Paul after alley-oop dunks, Jordan would get barked at if he committed a simple mistake.

But if that was the case with DeAndre Jordan, the world will never know. Both players have said nothing but sweet words for each other since that incident and after their heart-to-heart talk in Jordan's home. This newfound respect, not just between Paul and Jordan, but Griffin included, should make the team much stronger this coming season. The Clippers' game has always been up-tempo and high-octane. Without Jordan's defense and rebounds, Chris Paul would not have the ball much in his hands to create basketball plays.

On the contrary, some may even argue that Jordan's rise as one of the top centers in the league was because of Chris Paul in most part. DJ was never a player with a lot of offensive moves inside the paint. However, he dominated not because of skills but because of his ability to finish strong when given an opening. And, of course, DeAndre Jordan found a lot of open looks because Chris Paul was out there creating for him. With Jordan going back to the Clippers, the winning should continue. Hopefully it will get them past Round 2 of the playoffs this time around.

With some unfamiliar faces on his team, Chris Paul focused on trying to get his new team integrated into the offense in the first few games of the season. Paul's primary motive was to give as much confidence to the new acquisitions as possible. To accomplish that, he made it a point to share the ball on offense while taking fewer shots than he was accustomed to. Initially, the plan worked as the Los Angeles Clippers started the 2015-16 season going undefeated in their first four games.

After starting the 2015-16 season with a 4-0 streak, the Clips went on to lose 7 of their next ten games, primarily because of lineup changes with the injury of J.J. Redick. Moreover, they were still integrating newcomers Paul Pierce and enigmatic wingman Lance Stephenson within the team's system. But as the season went on, it was clear that the new acquisitions were not as key in giving the Clippers the advantage they sorely needed in a difficult Western Conference setup.

Instead of trying new things they were not familiar with, the Clippers once again sought to rely on the brilliance of Chris

Paul in getting the team back to playoff contention. In December, the star point guard went back to his usual ways of getting his teammates open by himself instead of allowing other players to make plays. The results were fantastic for both the Clippers and Paul, who would have nine double-doubles in that month.

Just when the Los Angeles Clippers were trying to get on a roll in the middle of the season, tragedy struck the roster. Never the healthiest team in the NBA in the last few seasons, the Clippers would lose their leading scorer Blake Griffin because of a partially torn quad he suffered versus the Lakers on December 25. The injury would sideline the athletic big man for the majority of the season. Griffin would not return to the lineup until the season was about to end in April 2016.

What the injury meant for the Clippers was that they were going to lose their best big men and top scorer. Aside from being able to make plays for others, Griffin was one of the top recipients of Chris Paul's passes and was his best option on offense. Because of the injury to Griffin, the LA Clippers were without their most explosive scorer and their secondary playmaker.

Without Griffin, Chris Paul was forced to shoulder more of the load for the LA Clippers, similar to how he singlehandedly led the New Orleans Hornets back in his days in the Big Easy. Not only did Paul dominate the playmaking duties more often than he already did, but he was also forced to handle more scoring duties for the Clippers, who were sorely missing their leading scorer.

With Chris Paul shouldering the burden of the Clippers, the team went on a 10-game winning streak highlighted by several of CP3's marvelous performances. He had six double-doubles in that winning stretch. Paul's best performance featured a 21-point, 19-assist blowout win against the Portland Trailblazers on January 6, 2016.

While the Clippers never replicated the same winning streak they enjoyed during that stretch from late December up to early January, they were able to maintain their competitive nature even without their second best player. It was all thanks to the extraordinary effort that Chris Paul was putting up on a nightly basis for the Los Angeles Clippers.

For his efforts in almost singlehandedly making the Los Angeles Clippers a contending team despite the injuries, the chemistry issues, and the wingman problems they were facing, Chris Paul was named an All-Star for the ninth consecutive and overall time in his already storied NBA career. His penchant for putting on a show was on full display during the All-Star Game as he finished with 14 points and a game-high 16 assists in only 19 minutes for the Western Conference team.

Chris Paul would get back to work in a big way a few weeks after the All-Star weekend concluded. In what seemed like his finest game of the season, CP3 finished a win in Sacramento with 40 points, eight rebounds, and 13 assists. He made 13 of his 20 shots including 4 of his nine three-point attempts in that game. While Paul seemed like he could not miss in that game, he never forgot to get his teammates involved in the action. He would play with the same kind of fire as a scorer and the same kind of unselfishness as a playmaker. The Los Angeles Clippers finished the regular season strong having won 10 of their final 12 games.

At the conclusion of the regular season, Chris Paul averaged 19.5 points, 4.2 rebounds, ten assists, and 2.1 steals. He was named to the All-NBA Second Team for the third time in his career. It was the eighth overall time that Paul was named an All-NBA selection. Aside from that, he made his eighth overall appearance in an All-Defensive Team and his sixth consecutive on the First Team. Getting consistently named to both the All-NBA and All-Defensive Teams meant that Chris Paul was indeed playing both ends of the court at elite levels.

While individual accolades and All-Team selections were proof of where Chris Paul stood among the many great point guards of his generation, his advanced statistics were what truly set him apart, even while younger and fresher playmakers were making trying to make a name in the NBA. Among all the other point guards in the league, Chris Paul was third in player efficiency rating. Only Stephen Curry and Russell Westbrook ranked higher than he did during the 2015-16 season.

However, Chris Paul was far ahead of those two superstars concerning assist ratio despite playing fewer minutes. The 32.7 minutes per game that Paul played that season was the lowest he had ever played in his career and yet his numbers still on par with his best seasons. Finally, CP3 was again third concerning estimated wins added to his team. Only Curry and Westbrook were ahead of him in that department. What those numbers meant for Paul was that he was still as elite of a point guard as he could be despite largely playing against bigger, younger, and more athletic counterparts. There was indeed no denying how great of a player Chris Paul is.

Thanks to the near superhuman efforts of CP3 in leading the offensive charge of his team, the Los Angeles Clippers made one of the top spots in the Western Conference. With a record of 53 wins as against 29 losses, the Clippers were the fourth seed in the West and were assured home court advantage in the first round of the postseason. They were able to accomplish such a feat even without Blake Griffin thanks to Chris Paul's leadership abilities.

Coming into the playoffs, the Los Angeles Clippers were the clear favorites in their first round matchup against the Portland Trailblazers, who were relying just as much on their star point guard as the Clips were that season. LAC was the more complete and healthier team in that series, and they proved to be the superior squad in the first two meetings.

In Game 1 of their series against the Blazers, Chris Paul went back to where he left off during the regular season. He torched Damian Lillard's defense while thoroughly outplaying the high-scoring point guard. Paul contributed to a blowout 20-point win with 28 points, six rebounds, and 11 assists. Game 2 was not a different story as Paul proved to be the superior point guard once again. Compared to Lillard's 17 points, CP3 finished with 25 points en route to a 21-point win over the Clippers.

While Chris Paul was putting up his usual elite numbers in Game 3, Damian Lillard finally snapped out of his personal shooting slump by scoring 32 points as against CP3's 26. Lillard's efforts were just enough to get the Blazers within one game away from the Los Angeles Clippers, who seemed like they were going to breeze through to the second round with an easy series win.

Just when the Clippers were intent on making it a 3-1 series in their favor with a win in Game 4, fate reared her ugly head to the dismay of the Los Angeles squad. In the middle of a hotly contested fourth game, Chris Paul was forced to leave the game early because of a broken hand. He would only play 24 minutes in that sorry loss to the Portland Trailblazers, who took advantage of the superstar point guard's absence to tie the series 2-2.

But Chris Paul's injury was not the only misfortune that the Clips faced in that game. They would also lose Blake Griffin yet again. Because of that, the Los Angeles Clippers were forced to play out the rest of the series without their two best players. And though the team was able to survive without Griffin during the majority of the regular season, it was doubtful that they could put up a good fight without Chris Paul, who carried the team on his back the entire year.

Because of the injury that Chris Paul suffered in Game 4, the Los Angeles Clippers would see their season ending in Game 6 in Portland. As expected, they seemed lost on the floor without their leader and best player. It was as if Chris Paul, whose body finally gave in because he had to carry the team on his back the entire season, was the sole player that kept the Clippers afloat.

Little did the world know that the injury to Chris Paul not only spelled doom for the Clippers in that series against the Blazers, but it also changed the entire playoff landscape in the Western Conference. The top-seeded team, the Golden State Warriors, were trying to survive the playoffs without their MVP Stephen Curry, who was nursing an injured knee.

After getting through the Rockets in the first round, the Warriors decided to keep their star point guard out of the lineup in the second round against the Portland Trailblazers in the hopes that they could beat their opponents while making sure their MVP was in top shape. While it was not an easy task, the Golden State Warriors defeated the Portland Trailblazers to proceed to the Conference Finals. Imagine if Damian Lillard and the Trailblazers had been Chris Paul and the Clippers.

While there is no denying the excellent work that Lillard and his team put together that season, Paul and his squad were undoubtedly the better ones. With or without Griffin, the Clippers had been playing their best brand of basketball because of the leadership of Chris Paul. There was no doubt that their level of play would have remained the same had they been the ones that made it to the second round against the Warriors instead of the Blazers.

Had Chris Paul been healthy the entire postseason, the world could have finally witnessed the Clippers getting past the second round. With Stephen Curry out of the lineup for the Warriors because of injury, Paul would have dished out his best against the backup playmakers of Golden State. There was no denying that he would have torched the Warrior backcourt with Curry out of the lineup. Paul's competitive drive could have even been enough to send the Los Angeles Clippers to the Western Conference Finals. But, as we all know now, it was not meant to be. Chris Paul and the Clippers would have to wait one more season to get a chance to force their way out of the second round once more.

Chapter 5: Paul's International Basketball Career

USA Basketball Chairman and Basketball National Team Managing Director Jerry Colangelo held a two-day mini-camp from August 11-13, 2015, in Las Vegas to determine the participants for Team USA in the 2016 Rio Olympics. The mini-camp was attended by 34 players, including eight new additions to the National Team's original roster. Chris Paul was among eight players from the 2012 London Olympic team who participated in the light workouts and drills. While the two-day camp was just the prelude to a more tedious selection process, it already showed Coach K which players wanted to commit themselves seriously to playing for the flag.

Along with Chris Paul came Clippers' teammates Blake Griffin and DeAndre Jordan. Griffin was supposed to be Paul's teammate on the 2012 Olympic team, but pulled out because of a knee injury. Paul said it would be very special for him and the Clippers' franchise as a whole if the three of them could play together on the 2016 USA Men's' Basketball team. It was, however, not meant to be for Chris Paul or Blake Griffin. Because they were nursing the injuries they both faced during the 2016 playoffs, both Paul and Griffin had to beg off from the

Olympics, though they would have most likely been part of Team USA because of their experience and sheer talent. Only DeAndre Jordan made the cut out of the three prospective Clippers that could have played for the team.

It was disappointing not to see Chris Paul donning the USA colors in the 2016 Olympics. Team USA sorely missed their best playmaker and best pure point guard as they often struggled to get open shots for their uber-talented scorers. As seen from the past Olympics and FIBA tournaments that Paul participated in, no other American could make plays nearly as good as he did.

In London, it was Paul, Williams, and Russell Westbrook. Paul was again the best point guard in the lineup when they won the gold medal. During the 2014 FIBA Worlds, Coach K had Stephen Curry, Kyrie Irving, and Derrick Rose. When Paul first played for Team USA in the 2006 World Championships in Japan, he finished with a tournament best 44 total assists for the bronze medal-winning Americans.

In 2008, Paul was one of Coach K's key reserves and played a significant role in the gold medal game against Spain by scoring 13 points. In 2012, Paul was promoted to the starting PG position, where he averaged 8.3 points, 2.5 rebounds, 5.1 assists, and 2.5 steals per game in 25.8 minutes of playing time. Chris Paul did not play in the 2014 World Championships, but that was because he was bothered by injuries and there was word back then that Paul was to be rested by USAB for the 2016 Olympics.

Unfortunately, Paul could not make it to the Rio Olympics because of the injuries he was nursing. Had he been healthy enough, he would have been a sure pick for one of the backcourt spots. More likely than not, Chris Paul would have been the starting point guard for Team USA as he would have been thriving in finding guys like Klay Thompson, Kevin Durant, and Carmelo Anthony for easy open shots. Nevertheless, Paul is still in the prime of his playing years, and could still be one of the top picks that could make the cut in future editions of Team USA.

Chapter 6: Paul's Personal Life

Chris Paul's wife Jada Crawley was his college sweetheart. The couple wed on September 10, 2011, and played together on the long-running game show The Family Feud in November 2011. The Pauls have two children named Christopher Emmanuel Paul II and Camryn Alexis Paul, who were born on May 23, 2009, and August 16, 2012, respectively. They live in a Mediterranean-style mansion in Bel-Air that CP3 brought from pop singer Avril Lavigne for $8.5M in 2012.

Chris Paul has had a great deal of luck in his life. He grew up in a loving family with both parents, was blessed with the athleticism needed to make it into the NBA despite his small frame, and was raised in an environment that encouraged his basketball skills without burning him out. Thanks to his background, Paul has been a leader for his entire life both on and off the basketball court. In August 2013, Paul was elected president of the NBA Players Association, the labor union, after four years of service on the NBPA's executive committee. The Players Association had been severely frayed due to poor management and had shown themselves to be highly ineffective during the 2011 NBA lockout. Paul's election brought credibility to the union, and while his tenure remains short, he showed effective leadership during the Donald Sterling crisis.

In addition to being the cheap, incompetent owner of Chris Paul's Clippers, Sterling had a well-known racist background. In 2014, Sterling was recorded making openly racist statements and disparaging all-time NBA great Magic Johnson. When the recording was publicly distributed, Paul quickly denounced Sterling. While such an action would be expected, Paul then organized the Clippers to boycott Game 5 of the first round of the 2014 NBA Playoffs against the Golden State Warriors. None of the Clippers wanted to miss a playoff game in such a close series, but they understood the importance of sending a message against Sterling. Fortunately, NBA Commissioner Adam Silver banned Donald Sterling from the league for life. The threat of a boycott from NBA players like Paul was undoubtedly a contributing factor, and Paul expressed his satisfaction with Silver's response. The Clippers had been blown out in Game 4 in the Warriors arena, certainly distracted by Sterling's remarks. But when they took the floor in Game 5, they saw the Clippers fans wearing black and chanting the message, "We are one," to counter what Sterling said. No one was prouder of that moment than Paul, who nearly broke down into tears.

Chris Paul is also a leader when it comes to humanitarian work. Even when he was on his rookie contract, Paul founded the CP3 Foundation, a charity that seeks to "enhance and promote education, health, sports and social responsibility for youth and families." The CP3 Foundation has worked with groups like Habitat for Humanity and Meals on Wheels to provide a better life for the less fortunate. The CP3 Foundation assisted in the rebuilding of New Orleans after Hurricane Katrina and worked together with Chase Bank to create the CP3 Afterschool Zone, which provides a place for schoolchildren to stay and live a productive lifestyle after the class day is done.

While Paul played football and basketball as a child, today his great passion is bowling. In November 2012, the Professional Bowlers' Association (PBA) decided to form a PBA League, which features eight teams set up in different cities like NBA franchises. Chris Paul quickly moved to buy the Los Angeles PBA franchise, declaring how excited he was to meet some of the best PBA bowlers. He is also a spokesperson for the United States Bowling Congress. As part of the CP3 Foundation, Paul has also run a charity bowling tournament every year since 2008, which has included NBA stars such as Blake Griffin, LeBron James, and Kevin Durant. In 2013, the tournament was even aired on ESPN! While Paul may love to relax with a game of bowling, there is no doubt that when he is focused on things like basketball or charity, he is willing to give it his all.

Charity work is not the only example of Chris Paul's heart. The love that Paul had for his beloved "Papa Chilly" was discussed earlier, and even after he became an NBA superstar, his 61 points in high school to honor his grandfather remains his most emotional moment. But despite his love for his grandfather—or perhaps because of it—he has stated that he wishes that the perpetrators of the crime, all of whom are behind bars today, would be released. The teenagers who murdered Papa Chilly were tried as juveniles, and three of them will be released in 2016 or 2017. But two of them were sentenced to life in prison, and despite's Paul wishes, will likely never walk out as free men. Nevertheless, more than bowling tournaments or charity work, Chris Paul's willingness to forgive those who wronged him so badly shows his generosity and the sincerity of his heart.

As the best basketball player on the best NBA team in basketball-crazy Los Angeles, Chris Paul has also become a global icon with his share of advertisements and sponsors. But unlike many NBA athletes who are known for their sponsorships of sneakers and sports drinks, Chris Paul's best-known ads have been for the State Farm Insurance Company. In these advertisements, Chris Paul has a twin brother, nerdy mustachioed "Cliff" Paul, who, like Chris Paul, is "born to assist" others. Cliff Paul has become a celebrity of his own, showing up at the NBA All-Star Game for interviews. In one postgame press conference, even coach Doc Rivers accidentally referred to Chris as "Cliff!" Outside of his State Farm sponsorship, Paul also has sponsorship deals with Nike and Powerade. He also appeared as the cover player for the NBA 2K8 video game. In 2014, Chris Paul was ranked by Forbes as one of the top-earning athletes with estimated earnings of $24.2M, which included some $5.5M in sponsorship and advertisement deals.

Chapter 7: Impact on Basketball

To discuss Chris Paul's basketball impact is to come face to face with a great contradiction when we talk about NBA players. While everyone acknowledges that basketball is a team sport, we also decide the individual legacies of players by whether that individual player "won" or "lost." We do this even while we acknowledge that the team is what really won or lost, and cover up that contradiction with emotional narratives like "will" and "heart."

As mentioned earlier, Chris Paul, by the standards of advanced statistics, is arguably one of the greatest point guards in the history of the NBA. It is one thing to discuss whether that is necessarily a good argument because there are many concerns about advanced statistics. However, one of the counterpoints that are frequently used to dismiss Chris Paul is the fact that he has not won much compared to many of the all-time greats.

As of the time of this writing, Chris Paul has never been past the second round of the NBA playoffs. He has won division titles, received All-Star and All-NBA nominations year after year, but he has never achieved real playoff success. He has never won a playoff series as an underdog, and in fact, has lost a playoff series where he was expected to win, namely the 2013 defeat to the Memphis Grizzlies in the first round. He was also part of a team that squandered away a 3-1 lead in the second round to eventually lose the series after leading the game that would have sent him to the Conference Finals. How could such a point guard be one of the best ever to play in the NBA?

The answer comes down to a fact which everyone knows, but frequently do not acknowledge: while an NBA star has a bigger impact in his sport compared to an NFL or MLB star, he can only do so much against five other players. This is particularly the case for a point guard. Chris Paul can thread the best pass in the world to a wide-open shooter or a big man underneath the rim. But if the shooter misses or the big man cannot catch the ball because his hands are clumsy, that pass becomes meaningless. When Chris Paul was with the New Orleans Hornets and had players like Peja Stojakovic, Tyson Chandler, and David West, he led the Hornets farther than anyone had ever expected from them. But when Chandler and Stojakovic succumbed to injuries, West began to age, and the replacements proved inadequate, there was only so much Paul could do. He was good enough to lead them to the playoffs when healthy, but once there, the Hornets lost to superior talent, better coaching, or both.

When Paul joined the Clippers, the expectation was that he and Griffin would eventually lead Los Angeles to that elusive ring. But so far, he has been held back by the difficulty of playing in the Western Conference. Despite Paul's numerous challenges over the years, history offers few excuses to those who fail. Despite injuries and the setback with Donald Sterling, the 2014-15 Clippers were the best team in the franchise's history. So Chris Paul will need to take them where they have never gone and where he has never gone—the Conference Finals at least, and a ring at best.

But, as history would tell us, Chris Paul has yet to deliver the goods and the hardware for his team despite playing with a lot of talented and experienced players. While his lack of effort could not be faulted for the missing ring on his finger, Paul's overall health has been a factor as to why the Clippers could never get over the hump in the playoffs. Because CP3 was forced to carry the team on so many different occasions, he was often banged up and tired coming into the postseason.

Nevertheless, there is just too much talent, leadership, and competitiveness in Chris Paul's 6-foot frame to imagine him going down in NBA history as a ring-less superstar. He is arguably the best pure point guard of his generation and yet the championship trophy often found a way to elude him. But the thought of one day seeing CP3 hoisting the championship trophy is not a far-fetched idea given the sheer talent and skill that the star point guard has as he continues to lead his team to greater heights.

Chapter 8: Paul's Legacy and Future

Not since the time of Isiah Thomas have we seen a small point guard with as much heart, skill, competitive edge, and drive to win that Chris Paul has. At 6-feet tall, Chris Paul may not be the biggest at his position, but he trumps all of his other matchups because of his talent, dedication, and willingness to win. It was the same kind of talent, dedication, and desire that we saw in Thomas when he was leading the 80's edition of the Detroit Pistons to the top of the NBA.

Like Thomas, Paul has won numerous individual awards and All-NBA selections. They have both seen their share of All-Star appearances. However, what set Isiah apart from CP3 were the two championships he won playing in one of the toughest eras in basketball history. Unlike Chris Paul, Isiah Thomas has the hardware to prove that he is one of the greatest point guards in league history. Those championships that Thomas won were always what eluded Paul in his quest to become one of the greatest to have ever played the point guard spot.

Chris Paul may not have a great history of winning. He continues to bow out of the second round of the playoffs even with such a talented team. The Clippers are deeper than ever, Paul has the best coach of his career, and his second option,

Blake Griffin, has shown himself to be a superstar in his rights. But even with Los Angeles's improvement, the Clippers are still not favored to win the NBA title, especially because of the Spurs, the Thunder, and the Warriors. Nevertheless, Paul still has enough talent and veteran players with him to be able to have a monumental Conference Finals appearance.

Paul is still one of the best point guards in the league and one of the most competitive players in the world. But no matter what statistics Chris Paul puts up night after night, no matter how well he leads the Clippers, and no matter how many individual awards he obtains, Chris Paul's legacy will be determined by championship rings. A player's legacy can change so much with just one ring. Dirk Nowitzki's reputation went from being considered a choker who failed the Dallas Mavericks in the 2007 NBA Playoffs to a clutch performer and one of the greatest players in the history of the game when he won in 2011.

In the early 1990s, Hakeem Olajuwon was viewed as no better than centers like Patrick Ewing, David Robinson, and Brad Daugherty. After winning two titles, Hakeem is viewed far more positively than any of those centers. David Robinson's advanced statistics are arguably far better than Hakeem's, but Robinson's legacy is defined by Olajuwon's playoff victory over him in 1995. Whether it is better to rank players one way or another way is not the point here. Reality dictates that winning is how we decide who the best players are. Therefore, if Chris Paul is to place himself as an all-time great point guard, he must win.

The other question that will confront Paul in the future is how long he can hold onto the title of best point guard in the league. Arguably, Paul no longer holds that title because Steph Curry just won an MVP in 2015 and was named the league's first unanimous winner of that award in 2016. But Paul has been the best point guard longer than anyone else in the league has. He has been playing at an elite level ever since he stepped onto an NBA court.

Since his near-MVP season in 2008, Paul has been the gold standard that all other point guards are compared to. Fellow 2005 NBA Draft point guard Deron Williams challenged Paul for years and repeatedly beat him in head-to-head matchups. But Deron Williams has fallen off over the years, as he now lacks the explosiveness that he used to overpower the smaller Paul. Derrick Rose won the MVP in 2011 but has never been the same thanks to multiple knee injuries. Stephen Curry has lit up the league with his 3-point shooting and has won an MVP and a championship.

Both Westbrook and John Wall have unparalleled speed and athleticism, and there are more great young point guards today than perhaps at any moment in NBA history. You could include guys like Damian Lillard, Kyle Lowry, Kemba Walker, and Kyrie Irving into that conversation. But while Chris Paul may lack their youth and athleticism, no point guard in the league has his on-court knowledge. Eventually, one of those younger point guards will surpass the aging Paul, as time devours all things. Steph Curry has already marked his name above Paul, but whether he can remain on top as long as Paul did remains unanswered.

Even though Paul is aging and losing his title as the best point guard, he remains one of the best players in the league, especially with how much he has meant to the two franchises he has played for. He is arguably the best player in the history of the New Orleans Hornets (now Pelicans). He is the franchise's second-leading scorer. He also leads New Orleans history, by far, in assists and steals. Other than leading New Orleans in a lot of statistical categories, CP3 also led them to multiple playoff appearances. His best season with the franchise was in 2008 when he almost won the MVP and led the team to a second seed in the West. With only a few superstars in the franchise's history, only Anthony Davis is capable of surpassing Chris Paul as the best player in New Orleans' history.

With the Clippers, who are also known to have had only a few notable players in their history, Chris Paul is arguably already the best point guard on Los Angeles' second team. Since joining the team in 2011, CP3 has become the second best passer in Clippers history and is currently third in steals. Paul is also highest in franchise assists with 9.9 assists per game and also in steals per game with 2.3. Overall, Paul has been the most efficient player in Clippers history with 26.1.

Without a doubt, Chris Paul is the best point guard in Clippers history and could very well be the best player to wear the team's uniform. His running mate Blake Griffin is the only other player who could be argued as the better Clipper player in history since the Clips were never known to be a very successful franchise with superstars. If the duo could win a title, there will be no doubt about their place in Clippers history.

The legacy of Chris Paul will still be written in the next few years as his prime begins to reach its end. Will the point guard who puts up incredible numbers and leads a team night in and night out be able to secure that elusive championship? Will Paul achieve his rank among the greatest point guards? And how long will this point guard be able to dominate his position? Until that day comes when someone surpasses him, this generous, intelligent man who has endured terrible and horrific losses will showcase himself as possibly the greatest point guard there ever was and ever will be alongside greats like Magic Johnson, John Stockton, and Isiah Thomas.

Final Word/About the Author

I was born and raised in Norwalk, Connecticut. Growing up, I could often be found spending many nights watching basketball, soccer, and football matches with my father in the family living room. I love sports and everything that sports can embody. I believe that sports are one of most genuine forms of competition, heart, and determination. I write my works to learn more about influential athletes in the hopes that from my writing, you the reader can walk away inspired to put in an equal if not greater amount of hard work and perseverance to pursue your goals. If you enjoyed *Chris Paul: The Inspiring Story of One of Basketball's Greatest Point Guards,* please leave a review! Also, you can read more of my works on *Brett Favre, Calvin Johnson, Drew Brees, J.J. Watt, Colin Kaepernick, Aaron Rodgers, Peyton Manning, Tom Brady, Russell Wilson, Michael Jordan, LeBron James, Kyrie Irving, Klay Thompson, Stephen Curry, Kevin Durant, Russell Westbrook, Anthony Davis, Chris Paul, Blake Griffin, Kobe Bryant, Joakim Noah, Scottie Pippen, Carmelo Anthony, Kevin Love, Grant Hill, Tracy McGrady, Vince Carter, Patrick Ewing, Karl Malone, Tony Parker, Allen Iverson, Hakeem Olajuwon, Reggie Miller, Michael Carter-Williams, John Wall, James Harden, Tim Duncan, Steve Nash, Draymond Green, Kawhi Leonard, Dwyane Wade, Ray Allen,*

Pau Gasol, Dirk Nowitzki, Jimmy Butler, Paul Pierce, Manu Ginobili, Pete Maravich, Larry Bird, Kyle Lowry, Jason Kidd, David Robinson, LaMarcus Aldridge, Derrick Rose, Paul George, Kevin Garnett, Chris Paul and Marc Gasol in the Kindle Store. If you love basketball, check out my website at claytongeoffreys.com to join my exclusive list where I let you know about my latest books and give you lots of goodies.

Like what you read? Please leave a review!

I write because I love sharing the stories of influential people like Chris Paul with fantastic readers like you. My readers inspire me to write more so please do not hesitate to let me know what you thought by leaving a review! If you love books on life, basketball, or productivity, check out my website at claytongeoffreys.com to join my exclusive list where I let you know about my latest books. Aside from being the first to hear about my latest releases, you can also download a free copy of *33 Life Lessons: Success Principles, Career Advice & Habits of Successful People*. See you there!

Clayton

References

[i] "My Amazing Journey—Chris Paul". *NBA.com*. 2007. Web

[ii] "Chris Paul". *JockBio*. Web

[iii] "Chris Paul". *NBA Draft*. Web

[iv] "Chris Paul". *DraftExpress*. Web

[v] "Chris Paul". *DraftExpress*. Web

[vi] "Chris Paul". *DraftExpress*. Web

[vii] "Report: Hornets Star Paul Wants Trade". *Fox Sports*. 22 July 2010. Web

[viii] Buha, Jovan. "Effects of CP3 Vetoed Trade Being Felt Four Years After the Proposed Move". *Fox Sports*. 8 December 2015. Web

38587741R00080

Made in the USA
Middletown, DE
22 December 2016